D0104899

STEVE NASH

THE MAKING OF AN MVP

JEFF RUD

WITH A FOREWORD BY STEVE NASH

PUFFIN BOOKS

PUFFIN BOOKS

Published by the Penguin Group
Penguin Young Readers Group,
345 Hudson Street, New York, New York 10014, U.S.A.
Penguin Group (Canada), 90 Eglinton Avenue East, Suite 700, Toronto, Ontario, Canada M4P 2Y3
(a division of Pearson Penguin Canada Inc.)
Penguin Books Ltd, 80 Strand, London WC2R 0RL, England
Penguin Ireland, 25 St Stephen's Green, Dublin 2, Ireland (a division of Penguin Books Ltd)
Penguin Group (Australia), 250 Camberwell Road, Camberwell, Victoria 3124, Australia
(a division of Pearson Australia Group Pty Ltd)
Penguin Books India Pvt Ltd, 11 Community Centre,
Panchsheel Park, New Delhi - 110 017, India
Penguin Group (NZ), 67 Apollo Drive, Mairangi Bay, Auckland 1311, New Zealand
(a division of Pearson New Zealand Ltd.)
Penguin Books (South Africa) (Pty) Ltd, 24 Sturdee Avenue,
Rosebank, Johannesburg 2196, South Africa

Registered Offices: Penguin Books Ltd, 80 Strand, London WC2R 0RL, England

First published in Canada by Puffin Canada, a division of Pearson Canada Inc., 2006
First published in the United States of America by Puffin Books,
a division of Penguin Young Readers Group, 2007

1 3 5 7 9 10 8 6 4 2

Copyright © Jeff Rud, 2006
All rights reserved
CIP Data is available.

Puffin Books ISBN 978-0-14-241014-1

Printed in the United States of America

*For my grandfather Cliff, who I'm certain
would have been a Steve Nash fan*

CONTENTS

FOREWORD

BY STEVE NASH

One of my all-time best basketball memories didn't happen in U.S. Airways Center, or Madison Square Garden, or Staples Center. It came on the floor of the aging Agrodome in Vancouver on March 14, 1992, the night we won the British Columbia High School championship.

It was the first—and the only, I hate to admit—basketball team I have ever played on that won its final game of the post-season. Capturing a provincial championship for St. Michaels University School was one of the most satisfying experiences of my life to date. And before I'm through playing the game, I hope to experience a similar feeling at the NBA level.

I remember looking around at all the guys on that high school team, at our coach Ian Hyde-Lay, and thinking how lucky I was to be a part of something so special. Nearly fifteen years later, I still feel the same way. I still count on "Hydes" for advice and guidance, and I still count those SMUS teammates as lifelong friends. The same goes for the kids I began the game with at Arbutus Junior Secondary, where Dave "Lanny" Thomson and Mike Sheffer opened up the gym for us on too many weekends to remember. For three years, we practically lived in that Arbutus gym. It's where we learned to love the game.

All of us in this world are a combination of our experiences, and I've been fortunate to have had plenty through the years that have shaped me as a player and as a person. Most have been positive, a few negative, but each one of them was valuable in some way. You'll find the key ones well documented in this book.

My mom and dad were always tremendously supportive, often sacrificing their own time and comforts so that my brother Martin, sister Joann, and I could pursue all of our sports and hobbies and friendships. Our house in Gordon Head was always a place where kids were welcome and encouraged to succeed.

I'm sure I inherited some athletic ability from my dad, John, although his first choice for me would have been soccer. In fact, during my college career at Santa Clara, he joked that he should have cut off all my fingers when he had the chance. (At least I think he was joking.)

Maybe the most important thing I inherited from my parents, though, was a work ethic. They taught all three of us that when you start something, you finish it. They also taught us that the only way to improve at anything is through an honest effort. I guess those lessons always stuck with me.

If I had to pick one reason why I made it to the NBA, that would probably be it.

I worked hard. I always tried to have a ball in my hand and I maximized my time on the court.

Yes, there were times when I didn't feel like practicing, but I pushed myself to go back to the gym or the playground because I believed that it would pay off down the road. On June 26, 1996, the night I was drafted into the NBA, I thought about all those extra practice sessions.

That approach has also paid off for me in the NBA. I try to add something new to my game every season and—knock on wood—try to come up with better ways to keep my thirty-something body in good enough shape to withstand another hundred or so games of pounding. So far, so good.

There are so many positives about being a pro basketball player that it's hard to know where to start. Obviously, the money makes for a comfortable lifestyle, and it's a tremendously exciting challenge to test yourself against such incredible athletes on a nightly basis. The thing that is best about it, though, is that it puts you in a position where you can help a lot of people. Through the Steve Nash Foundation, which we began in 2001, we are thrilled to be able to assist "underserved" children in their health, personal development, education, and enjoyment of life. I am proud of the work of the foundation and grateful for all the support we have received from around the world. I believe we are making a difference and helping kids who both need and deserve it. There is nothing more gratifying than that.

I'm not really comfortable with the "celebrity" status that is projected onto professional athletes, however. I believe there are plenty of other people in the world more worthy of emulating than somebody who can dribble the ball or dunk or shoot a three-pointer. And it never ceases to amaze me how much attention people pay to silly things. My hair, for instance.

At the same time, I understand why kids look up to athletes. I remember idolizing Glenn Hoddle of Tottenham when I was a young boy. And to this day, I remain a faithful Spurs supporter.

Later, after I began concentrating more on basketball in junior high, I admired Isiah Thomas and Magic Johnson and, like every other kid back then, Michael Jordan. I devoured all the stories about them in newspapers, magazines, and books and listened to their interviews on television. I hung on their words.

My story is much different from those of the heroes I had growing up, but if young readers can find similar inspiration in these pages, it is well worth telling.

Steve Nash

PREFACE

More than a dozen years have passed since the idea of writing a book about Steve Nash first occurred to me. Back in 1994, I was a sportswriter with the Victoria *Times Colonist* newspaper, and Nash was making his mark as a U.S. college basketball star with the Santa Clara Broncos.

I'd love to tell you that I saw it coming—that back then I could picture the day when Nash would be named the Most Valuable Player in the National Basketball Association, not once but twice, in consecutive years.

I'd love to tell you that I predicted he'd be a multiple NBA All-Star, lead the league in assists, become one of pro basketball's top three-point and free-throw shooters of all time, and eventually even become a household name—at least in hoop-crazy households—around the world.

Truth is, I can't make that claim.

The first time I actually met Steve Nash was in 1991, when he was in Grade 12. I had seen him play basketball and I already knew he was the best Canadian high school guard I had ever laid eyes on. The thing I remember most about that initial meeting was Steve's personality. The kid was bright-eyed, articulate, mature, and, above all else, confident.

But the NBA? That possibility didn't even begin to dawn on me that December afternoon, sitting in the bleachers of the dreary St. Michaels University School

Old Gym in suburban Victoria, British Columbia, as I interviewed Nash prior to a team practice.

He had already earned quite a reputation in B.C. high school basketball circles, but if you had told me that the skinny, six-foot-one kid beside me would one day be the MVP of the finest professional league on the planet, I might have laughed you out of the gym. For Canadians, those thoughts simply weren't on any kind of radar screen back then.

Nobody saw this coming—except perhaps one guy. Steve Nash always had a rock-solid confidence in himself. He knew he had some God-given talent; he knew he was willing and able to outwork just about everybody he came up against; he knew he could always count on his family for support and guidance. He firmly believed he had a shot at making the NBA, even back then.

That's why Steve tried so desperately to get a U.S. college to notice him; why he stayed at Santa Clara University even after his early college career was fraught with frustration; why he patiently paid his dues as a rookie in Phoenix, watching quietly as the Suns stock-piled All-Star point guards ahead of him; and why he was able to shake off the boos of disappointed fans during his darkest days in Dallas. From the time he was in Grade 8, he believed in his heart that he was capable of playing and even excelling in the NBA. And with that belief established, who knew what his limitations might be? Certainly Steve wasn't about to place any on himself.

Back in Steve Nash's high school days, there was something intangible about the kid who made you feel like you shouldn't ever count him out. So, after he began quietly making an impression on the NBA scouts as a junior at Santa Clara, I began thinking seriously about writing a book about the young man from Victoria.

Early in his senior college year, Nash was a projected first-round draft pick, and by then the book was in motion. After Steve was drafted fifteenth overall by the Phoenix Suns in June 1996, we did indeed collaborate to publish *Long Shot: Steve Nash's Journey to the NBA*.

Back then, Steve Nash was a feel-good, inspirational story: *Short Canadian kid battles adversity to make it into the highest hoops circuit in the world*. Little did I know that Steve's story was just getting started.

Days after that draft, Steve sat in his parents' living room and talked about what the future might bring. "I'm in the NBA now, so I'm relaxed," he told me that afternoon. "But now I'm setting new goals. I want to win championships. I want to be an All-Star.

"I want to do it all."

He didn't say he wanted to be a two-time NBA MVP. He didn't say he wanted to make it into the Basketball Hall of Fame, even though that is where his career is surely now heading. But you get the picture: the kid was confident in himself; in his ability to learn and improve; in his steadfast refusal to give up against the greatest of odds or challenges. There were times when few others shared that confidence, but that never seemed to matter. There were times when that confidence was tested, but they never seemed to last.

Of the goals that Nash listed that day in 1996, the only one that he has yet to realize, ten years later, is winning an

NBA championship. He has led his various teams—with a unique, fearless, whirling-dervish style—into three Western Conference finals; he has become a wealthy young man and a fan favorite worldwide. But he has yet to taste the game's sweetest team prize. And for a player like Nash, whose game and philosophy are deeply rooted in a team approach to basketball, a championship is the ultimate goal. Ask him and he'll tell you, it is the true measure of any professional athlete.

Whether he achieves that championship or not remains to be seen. But there's one thing I've learned from watching Steve Nash over the years: it's never wise to bet against him.

Steve's story was already a good one back in 1996, when he bucked all odds just to make it to the NBA. It's now a great one, and I am delighted to have the opportunity to tell it on these pages.

1

MAKING A MOVE

"It hurt, because that was the most important thing in my world—playing basketball games."

—Steve Nash, sidelined high school star, 1990–91

He could hardly believe his eyes. There, across the top of the Sports section in the Victoria *Times Colonist*, was the big, bold, impossible-to-miss headline: "High school hoop star switching allegiances."

Sixteen-year-old Steve Nash shook his head slowly. The lengthy newspaper article running below the headline was all about him. Word of his transfer from the neighborhood high school where he had started that fall to a nearby private school had obviously spread beyond the basketball community on Vancouver Island. And, just as obviously, the move was a big deal—big enough to make a splash in the local daily paper, at least.

"A high school sports season already riddled with controversy over interschool player moves heated up even more on Sunday when Steve Nash's family announced that the highly-touted multi-sport Grade 11 star is leaving Mount Douglas [Senior Secondary] School for St. Michaels University School ..." the story began. "Nash is one of the most heralded incoming Grade 11 basketball stars in many years ..."

As he read it over, the newspaper article seemed strange to Steve. He had been playing basketball at a high level for a few years now. He had been the Most Valuable Player in the 1990 British Columbia Junior Secondary School championships while leading his Arbutus Aztecs to a second-place finish in the province just eight months earlier. He was a B.C. Under-17 Summer All-Star Team starter at point guard, and he had already been identified as one the best incoming senior high school prospects in provincial history. But the *Times Colonist* had never carried huge headlines about any of those things. Now, for something that really had little to do with his performance on the basketball court, there was suddenly a major fuss being made in the local Sports section.

In a way, it felt good to see his name in print, to see himself identified as a top-rated player, but this headline was also troubling. His transfer had nothing to do with "switching allegiances." He still had a lot of friends at Mount Douglas, kids he had grown up with at Arbutus Junior Secondary and, before that, at Hillcrest Elementary, the neighborhood school next to his family's house. The transfer wasn't going to break those ties.

All Steve wanted to do was to give himself the best possible chance of earning a U.S. college basketball scholarship, and this move to St. Michaels University School was going to help. Why did people who didn't even know him care so much about where he went to high school, anyway?

Still, the newspaper story was nothing compared to the real drawback of his transfer. Over the past couple of weeks, a painful realization had gradually sunk in for Steve: he would almost certainly have to sit out his entire Grade 11 basketball season because of the move.

Soon after exploring the possibility of a transfer to St. Michaels, Steve and his parents had discovered that, according to B.C. high school sports eligibility rules, he would forfeit a basketball season if he switched schools now. The Nashes planned to appeal that ruling, but the chances of success were slim.

The newspaper story was now spelling it out for Steve—and everybody else in Greater Victoria—in stark black and white. "Rules stipulate that any athlete who transfers schools after October 15 is ineligible for that season's basketball schedule at his or her new school."

Missing the upcoming basketball season would be a huge price to pay, one the hoop-crazy teenager certainly wasn't thrilled about. But the alternative—staying on at Mount Douglas and trying to make things work there— no longer seemed like an option.

The transition from Grade 10 at Arbutus Junior Secondary to Grade 11 at Mount Douglas Secondary School had been difficult for Steve. The high school teachers expected students to take full responsibility for their studies, and the sixteen-year-old didn't have the discipline, or in some cases even the interest, to keep up with his work. Steve had fallen behind in several classes and done poorly on tests and assignments.

As report card time approached that fall, Steve was getting the sinking feeling that his parents would be disappointed when they saw his marks. He knew he was letting them down. But he realized he was letting himself down more than anyone else. If he wanted to fulfill his dream of playing basketball in the NCAA, he knew he'd have to be more successful in high school.

"They gave you a lot of responsibility at Mount Doug and I didn't really take that on academically," Steve recalls. "I don't think my enthusiasm for academics was there to start with. I think a lot of it was just my own lack of discipline."

John and Jean Nash's eldest son had been a solid, if unspectacular, student through elementary school and junior high. But when his first high school report card arrived home in November, Steve's highest mark was a C-plus. For the first time ever he'd received a D-minus, in Chemistry. His parents were worried.

The grades weren't the worst of it, however. The Nashes also discovered on this eye-opening report card that their son had been absent for thirty-three classes during the first two months of his Grade 11 year. Commitments with the school's soccer team accounted for some of the absences, but other days he had simply decided to cut, and when he wasn't in class he was sometimes discovered shooting baskets in the school gym.

For John and Jean Nash, the report card was a wake-up call. Although the Nashes hoped their eldest son could land the college basketball scholarship he so desperately sought, and perhaps even one day get his coveted shot at the NBA, their biggest concern was that Steve get the grades he needed to graduate from high school and get into university.

Outside the classroom, life at Mount Douglas had actually gotten off to a terrific start for Steve. Soccer had been Steve's first sports passion, and in November he'd led the Mount Douglas Rams to a British Columbia AAA soccer championship. He'd even been selected the MVP of the tournament, despite being just an eleventh-grader. But basketball was another story.

The new basketball coach at Mount Douglas was Dave Hutchings, a no-nonsense leader with fifteen years' experience and a high profile in the local basketball community. Over the summer, Hutchings had transferred to Mount Douglas from rival Oak Bay High School, where he had coached successful teams every winter in the Lower Vancouver Island Secondary School Athletic Association. The forty-one-year-old Hutchings had visions of transforming the Mount Douglas basketball program into a provincial powerhouse. In fact, before the season had even begun, he had held a press conference to announce that the team's name would be changing to the "Runnin' Rams," styled after the reigning U.S. college champion University of Nevada–Las Vegas "Runnin' Rebels."

On the surface, Nash and Hutchings looked like a natural fit—a uniquely talented young player absolutely driven to be the best, teamed with a dedicated coach who longed to start a U.S.-style dynasty at Mount Douglas that would be the envy of the British Columbia basketball scene. But instead, the chemistry between star player and coach fizzled from the start.

From the opening practice, Steve and his friends found Hutchings negative and inflexible, especially compared to the easy-going coaches they had played for in junior high. Early practice sessions were continually stopped by Hutchings, who demanded that players do push-ups as a form of punishment for making mistakes or not listening. The incoming Arbutus players already felt they were superior to the eight returning twelfth-graders who comprised the rest of the Mount Douglas roster, and that did nothing to help team spirit. After a few practices, some of the younger players began ignoring the coach's commands altogether.

To Steve, this was nothing like the positive atmosphere he'd enjoyed on the Arbutus team—a team that had very nearly won a provincial junior title with him at the controls. The Aztecs had finished the 1989–90 season with a 35–6 record and had fallen by just 4 points to cross-town rival Spencer Middle School only after Steve had fouled out with less than three minutes to go in the championship game.

The Arbutus grads who had moved up to Mount Douglas that fall were a tight-knit group who had played basketball almost every day for the past three years. Arbutus coaches Dave Thomson and Mike Sheffer had always been willing to open the gym for the boys on weekends and holidays for extra court time, and the guys would stay all day, leaving only long enough to skip across the street to teammate Mark Kennedy's house for food and then return to the court with handfuls of fruit and sandwiches. The group—led by Steve Nash, Jamie Miller, and Al Whitley—loved to play fast and hard, challenging each other in high-octane scrimmages, with the losers typically running laps or doing push-ups as penance. For Steve and his friends, the gym had quickly become a second home.

Dave Thomson had run a strong program at Arbutus for years, producing several university-caliber players. He believed in allowing his teams to play to their strengths. As he would put it, "If you have racehorses, you don't turn them into Clydesdales." The Aztecs' style was pressure defense, combined with running the ball down opponents' throats. But that didn't go over well with Hutchings. The new Mount Douglas coach liked his teams more disciplined, more methodical, more coach-driven. The young players got the distinct feeling that the coach was trying to break the bonds they had forged on and off the court during the past three years. And he obviously didn't believe these young boys could be successful playing the same run-and-gun game at the senior high school level, not even with their undeniable talent.

The Arbutus kids had assumed they would pick up in high school where they had left off in junior high. But the two distinctly different theories collided daily on the Mount Douglas practice floor during the pre-season, and Steve quickly recognized that it wasn't a good atmosphere for anybody.

What really soured the sixteen-year-old on playing for the coach, however, was one brief pre-season meeting.

Hutchings had asked each Mount Douglas player to visit his office individually for these sessions, during which they were supposed to establish goals, both for themselves and for the team in the coming season. Steve entered the coaches' office, located at the rear end of the massive Mount Douglas gym, eager to do just that.

"So what are your goals?" Hutchings asked.

"My goal is to play Division 1 basketball," Steve said confidently.

"Well, I think you might have to readjust your goals, Steve," Hutchings replied. "That's a pretty high level, and I think you should maybe make some more realistic goals."

As Steve Nash walked out of the coaches' office, he felt both stunned and angry. He had expected to hear a pep talk, to be offered some help, maybe even a constructive plan to land a Division 1 college scholarship over the next two years. Instead, he had simply been told "readjust your goals." From that moment, Steve began to seriously question whether he could play for Dave Hutchings. The continuing daily turmoil of practice simply reinforced that feeling.

And Steve's parents were not entirely happy with Hutchings, either. John Nash went to speak with the coach after Steve's disastrous report card came home. Hutchings told the concerned father that he shouldn't worry too much about the boy's grades—after all, if university didn't work out, Steve could always start his hoops career playing at a junior college. For the Nashes, this was simply not an option: basketball or no basketball, they wanted their son to get a university education.

Steve's parents were now looking into the possibility of a new school, and they weren't alone. Nancy Miller, whose son Jamie was one of Steve's best friends and a talented basketball teammate from Arbutus, also wanted her son to transfer out of Mount Douglas. The parents had heard from other friends that St. Michaels University School, a private school modeled on the traditional British preparatory schools, with a reputation for rigorous academic discipline and a lower teacher-to-student ratio, had worked well for their children. The campus was located just a few miles from their home.

It was worth a try, they reasoned, even though it would be costly. Steve's tuition for the remainder of his Grade 11 year would be $3,600, and another $6,800 would be required for his senior year. To make ends meet, the Nashes decided to sell their stake in a small appliance-repair business, and John, employed as a marketing manager by a local credit union, also took a part-time job coaching the St. Michaels soccer teams. Steve knew he wasn't the only one in the family who would be making sacrifices as a result of this move.

It was hard for Steve to leave behind his many good friends and teammates at Mount Douglas, but it helped that his close friend Jamie Miller was also making the move. Besides, this was his chance for a fresh academic start. And though he had spoken only briefly with Ian Hyde-Lay, Steve already felt comfortable with the earnest young SMUS basketball coach.

"I'd had such a bad start and a bad experience with the basketball program [at Mount Douglas] that it got to the point where it was kind of: 'Anywhere but here,'" Steve says now. "But I loved the school in some ways. I mean, we were B.C. soccer champs. I had good friends there. It's not something I necessarily wanted to do, but in the end, basketball was most important to me, and it wasn't a good place for that."

But if his transfer to St. Michaels was giving basketball back to Steve, it was also, if only temporarily, taking it away. For a kid who ate, slept, and breathed basketball, having to sit out his Grade 11 season was more painful than almost anything else he could have imagined. And considering that his immediate goal was to land a U.S. college scholarship, it was a devastating blow. As far as most U.S. college recruiters were concerned, Steve wouldn't even appear on the radar screen until his Grade 12 season. He could only hope that by then it wouldn't be too late.

The previous week, several days before the article in the *Times Colonist* appeared, word of Steve's and Jamie's pending transfer had begun to spread, and the boys had received their first experience of the fallout. They had planned to attend a U.S. college basketball exhibition series at Vancouver's B.C. Place Stadium with their Mount Douglas teammates. But once the school caught wind of the transfer, the boys were asked to make their own travel arrangements to and from the games.

Rumors had already begun circulating that Nash and Miller had been given scholarships to attend SMUS, that they had even received cars and cash as an inducement to make the switch. These stories were all untrue, but, as Steve was quickly finding out, that didn't stop them from spreading. People were saying that SMUS had recruited the two B.C. Summer All-Star Team members away from Mount Douglas in an attempt to "buy" a B.C. championship.

The rumors bothered the Nashes, who felt they were being labeled as cheaters by people who didn't know the first thing about them. They also bothered Ian Hyde-Lay, the coach and athletic director at SMUS, who had done nothing to encourage the boys to switch schools and who, in fact, had worried that the transfer might actually harm SMUS athletics because it would stir up hard feelings against private schools that always seemed to bubble just beneath the surface of B.C. high school sports.

"John Nash admitted that SMUS officials 'were wary' when he approached them about the transfer," the *Times Colonist* story continued. "'With all this recruiting controversy this year, everybody is afraid of being caught up in it, even if the whole thing is an honest academic move as it is in this case,' he said.... 'It's easy for talk to get out of hand, especially in this era of high school athletics, with everybody talking and spreading rumors that aren't true.'"

Steve surveyed the newspaper headline again. The date above it read Monday, December 3, 1990.

"The two students begin classes at SMUS today."

The word was definitely out, and the transfer was official. It was too late to turn back now.

2

IN GOOD HANDS

"I got to play for a terrific coach who taught me a lot, had a great eye for the game, and really saw things that other people didn't see—and that helped me a ton."

—Steve Nash, SMUS Blue Devil, 1991–92

Steve Nash sat on the end of the visitors' bench, just a few feet from the shiny floor in the familiar Mount Douglas Secondary School gymnasium. Beside him sat Jamie Miller, one of his best friends. The two lanky, athletic-looking boys easily stood out from the rest of their teammates because they weren't wearing basketball uniforms. Instead, they were attired in the formal blue blazers, dark slacks, white shirts, and neckties of their new private high school.

It was mid-January 1991, and this had become a familiar scene for Steve and Jamie. Since transferring to St. Michaels University School early in December, the two prominent members of the B.C. Under-17 Summer All-Star Team had been unable to play in any official games for their new school. For every SMUS Blue Devils game, at home or on the road, the boys' routine was now the same: find the end of the bench, have a seat, and watch their new teammates play.

This was one of the most frustrating experiences of Steve's young life. Since Grade 6 he had pictured himself playing high school basketball. Now he was finally there, so close to the hardwood he could reach out and tap the court with his black dress shoes, but he couldn't actually play.

This particular game, however, was a little different from the ones he and Jamie had watched from the bench so far. This was the first time SMUS had faced the Mount Douglas Runnin' Rams since the pair's controversial transfer to the private school. Tension was running high in the Mount Doug gym. Steve could feel it.

He was well aware how he and Jamie must look to the kids at Mount Douglas—at least the ones who didn't know them very well. They'd look like "snotty little private school snobs" coming back to thumb their noses at their old public school. *It's not true,* Steve thought to himself as he watched the game. *But we'd be thinking the same thing if it were somebody else in our place.*

The students in the Mount Douglas bleachers wasted little time responding to the presence of Steve and Jamie on the SMUS bench. Chants of "Traitors!" rung out across the huge gym as play began on the floor. But the two hundred or so SMUS students who had traveled to Mount Douglas to watch the game were ready. "We've got Nash and Miller!" they belted back in unison. "We've got Nash and Miller!"

Blue Devils coach Ian Hyde-Lay rushed from the bench to the front of the SMUS student section and urged them to be quiet. There were enough hard feelings about the transfer already. Nobody needed to fan the flames.

Steve Nash had long excelled at just about whatever he attempted athletically, including baseball, hockey, lacrosse, and especially soccer. In every sport he played, Steve was blessed with the ability to see the entire playing surface and quickly decide when and where best to move the puck or ball. Now nearly six-foot-one and an angular 165 pounds, Steve was quick and agile, with soft hands and outstanding footwork honed from hours on the soccer pitch with his father, John, a former professional player.

Steve had been introduced to basketball first in Grade 6 by Hillcrest Elementary coach Mike Gallo, who offered Wednesday-night scrimmage sessions at the gym located just across the playing field from the Nashes' comfortable family home.

Despite never having played the game before, Steve took to basketball quickly, seizing on Gallo's focus on fundamentals and working on them alone after his friends had gone home. Often, as Gallo was marking assignments in his classroom, he would hear the familiar sound of a bouncing ball and gaze out the window to the adjacent outdoor court. There, even on rainy afternoons, he would see his quiet but well-liked student running through a personal practice regimen. Steve was already using his left hand at a time when most players had trouble coaxing any consistent skills out of their right. Gallo couldn't help noticing that the kid was also working his way through a systematic routine: fifty right-handed lay-ups, fifty left-handed, twenty-five shots from the free-throw line, fifteen from each of the corners, dribbling drills with both hands.

In both practices and games at Hillcrest, Steve quickly developed a remarkable ability and desire to set up team-mates for easy scores, often with no-look passes far above the usual elementary school level of play. While he enjoyed scoring, he got a much bigger kick out of making the perfect assist and ensuring his team's success. At the midpoint of Grade 6, Steve was already the clear standout on the Hillcrest team, and before he graduated from Grade 7, Mike Gallo believed Nash had become perhaps the best basketball player in his age group in the entire city.

But although he showed early promise, Steve didn't really zero in on basketball until his Grade 8 year at Arbutus, as he and his buddies Al Whitley, Adam Miller, John Clancy, Mark Kennedy, and Jamie Miller became captivated by the NBA glamour era of Michael Jordan. After that, they practically lived on the outdoor basket-ball courts of their neighborhood during the spring and summer months, sharpening their games and mimicking their heroes' moves on the asphalt.

Once again, Steve's dedication went a step further than most of his buddies'. When there was no pickup game or even a one-on-one opponent to test himself against, he spent hours on the court alone, setting out tasks and then refusing to leave the playground until he had meticulously completed them, even if that meant going home in the dark. One day the goal might be to make five hundred jump shots, the next to sink two hundred free throws. Even as a young teenager, and even though it was only the playground, maximizing practice time was vitally important to Steve.

His workouts were not limited to the court, either. Steve taped basketball games featuring players he idolized, like Magic Johnson and Isiah Thomas. Then he broke down their individual moves—how Magic threw a left-handed no-look pass on the break or how Isiah blew by defenders with his cross-over dribble. After studying those moves over and over again on video, he headed to the hard court and tried to incorporate them into his workouts.

Even his daily walk to and from school was an opportunity to work on his ball-handling, with Steve sometimes dribbling a tennis ball to make the exercise more challenging. Over time, the basketball simply became an extension of either hand. And as he emerged as a junior high star for Arbutus in Grade 10, Steve Nash's ball-handling and passing skills had reached near-university levels.

Another characteristic that set Steve apart at this age was a willingness to work on his weaknesses. Arbutus coach Dave Thomson noticed early on that while other junior high players spent free time on the court doing things they were already proficient at, Steve used it to focus on the things he did worst. Steve had quickly recognized that using both hands was paramount to becoming a great basketball player, so he worked diligently on dribbling, passing, and shooting with his left hand. He became such a sophisticated passer that Thomson and Sheffer had to convince Steve that some of his teammates were simply not ready for the passes he was tossing their way.

While his skill level had grown quickly, Steve hadn't sprouted up to the physical heights that many of his basketball-playing friends were reaching. Entering high school, he had hovered around the six-foot mark—taller than most boys his age but still relatively short in the context of his favorite sport. As teenagers, Steve and his younger brother Martin had dutifully charted their growth on the back of a bedroom door, and Steve had even jokingly once asked his mother why she hadn't chosen a taller man to marry. But as he approached the six-foot-one mark in high school and was still growing, Steve knew that his stature wasn't the biggest obstacle for him to overcome, especially at the point guard position. While his height alone certainly wouldn't make him stand out for college recruiters, it also wouldn't stop them from considering him for a scholarship.

Not long after he truly set his sights on basketball, an eighth-grade Steve declared to his mother that he would one day play in the NBA. It was no idle boast. While his family, friends, and most coaches quietly supported his ambitions, Steve dove headlong into achieving them. They were "hoop dreams" to be sure, but with enough work, he had always been reasonably confident that they were attainable.

Now, with Ian Hyde-Lay as his new coach, Steve had found somebody he could both connect with personally and respect as an authority figure.

An intense thirty-two-year-old in only his first year as a high school head coach after taking over from longtime SMUS coach Bill Greenwell, Hyde-Lay recognized the tremendous potential of Steve Nash. Many others in the Victoria basketball community were by now well aware of the youngster's talents as well. In fact, by the time he transferred to SMUS, there was so much interest in Steve that his first practice with the Blue Devils attracted a crowd of about 150 students, curious to see what the fuss was all about.

But Ian Hyde-Lay differed from many who admired the youngster's basketball skills. The SMUS coach also had some definite thoughts about how Steve could improve his game, remove some of the unnecessary flash, and make it more disciplined and efficient.

The young coach was delighted to discover that Nash was a true "gym rat," a player who would happily spend hours on the court working to make himself a better player. Hyde-Lay was glad to oblige Steve by opening up the gym for weekend and early-morning one-on-one sessions, in which the pair worked on fundamentals such as footwork and shooting. Hyde-Lay had been a walk-on basketball player at the University of Victoria who'd worked hard enough at his game to become captain of the Canadian-champion Vikings by his senior year. He was a stickler for fundamentals and the mantra that "perfect preparation makes for perfect performance." He had played under legendary UVic coach Ken Shields, and he was now passing on many of the lessons he learned from Shields to his newest players.

"Try to be better today than you were yesterday and better tomorrow than you are today," Hyde-Lay would encourage Steve and Jamie as they worked together in the gym. In an address to Steve and other SMUS student athletes in the school yearbook, Hyde-Lay wrote: "Remember the value of loyalty, duty, unselfishness, and sportsmanship." To a lot of kids, this seemed like hokey stuff, but Steve quickly realized there was plenty of value in it as well.

While the teenage Nash's ball-handling skills were far above those of the average high school student, Hyde-Lay believed Steve often did too much with the ball in order to accomplish too little. He urged Steve to remove the hot-dog tendencies from his game, to become more efficient with the basketball instead of dribbling through his legs and around his back simply because he could.

Steve was talented enough that he could drift sideways on his jump shot and still regularly sink it. Hyde-Lay reinforced to the youngster the value of balanced shooting form, of keeping his eyes fixed on the hoop, of landing six inches farther up the court than where he began his shot, and of following through with his shooting hand to an almost ridiculously exaggerated degree after releasing the ball.

It was under Hyde-Lay, a perfectionist in the tradition of his mentor, that Steve began to fine-tune his deadly shooting stroke. Although the talented teen could already drive the ball to the hoop at will and finish with a crowd-pleasing assortment of lay-ups, Hyde-Lay painstakingly stressed to Steve the value of a simple full-speed, pull-up jump shot.

"Steve, you're going to be playing somewhere [in college] where every guy in the paint is going to be six-foot-nine and capable of jumping out of the gym," Hyde-Lay would tell his young star as he rebounded for him during these sessions. "What they can't stop is you stopping at the free-throw line and pulling up for the jumper."

Meanwhile, the connection to Ian Hyde-Lay was paying off for Steve in other ways. Not long after his seventeenth birthday, in the spring of 1991, Steve was invited by Ken Shields to practice with the Canadian senior men's team during a ten-day training camp at the University of Victoria.

Ken Shields was essentially the godfather of Canadian basketball. He had coached UVic to seven consecutive Canadian university titles in the 1980s and he was now in charge of the national men's programs. Due in large part to what he was hearing from Ian Hyde-Lay, the godfather was now making an offer that Steve Nash couldn't refuse.

Shields invited Steve to camp because his roster was short one guard, so it wasn't a formal tryout for the senior team. But allowing such a young player to compete in this kind of environment was an unprecedented move. Living in Victoria, Shields had seen enough of Nash himself, and had heard enough from Hyde-Lay, that he was confident the boy could handle the pressure and challenge of the situation.

So while he wasn't getting the benefit of a Grade 11 season, Steve was given an opportunity to get the kind of seasoning—testing his skills against veteran European players and even a few NBA pros—that extended far beyond the experience of the average high-schooler. And Ken Shields found himself marveling that the slender point guard, despite giving up several years' strength and size to the rest of the national team, did not look at all out of place during these workouts.

It was during a moment at this camp that the wisdom of Hyde-Lay's individual sessions clicked in for Steve. As the teenager drove the floor on a fast break during a scrimmage, seven-footer Mike Smrek of the Los Angeles Clippers lurked in the key, waiting for the point guard to attempt a lay-up so he could swat it away. Instead, Steve pulled up briskly at the free-throw line and drained a jumper. On his way up court, he flashed a huge, knowing grin at Hyde-Lay.

Ken Shields was also sufficiently impressed with Steve during that training camp to arrange a special trip for the teenager the following December. He and Ian Hyde-Lay took the seventeen-year-old to Seattle to attend a Seattle SuperSonics–Golden State Warriors NBA game. Shields made the arrangements through the Warriors, with whom he had been an observer-coach in training camp

that fall. Golden State assistant coach Donnie Nelson provided them with seats directly behind the Warriors' bench, so they could get a good look at the players.

The Golden State team wore long-sleeved warm-ups as they shot around before the game. Just prior to tip-off, as they peeled off their outer layers, Ken Shields nudged Steve. "Check out Hardaway," he said.

Steve's eyes bulged as he peered at the Warriors' star point guard, Tim Hardaway. The speedy veteran's body was chiseled through a routine of daily push-ups and weights. "If you want to play in the NBA," Shields told Steve, "that's the kind of body you've got to have." Steve now had a new measure for the kind of hard work and physical commitment that college basketball—and certainly the professional game—would call for.

While the lessons continued on the court, Ian Hyde-Lay was also instrumental in helping Steve to turn things around academically at SMUS. The coach insisted that all his players attend mandatory two-hour study hall sessions after practice four times a week, forcing them to complete their homework or study rather than putting it off. Hyde-Lay also followed through on discipline, at times suspending Steve from practice during that Grade 11 season when the teenager failed to complete school assignments on time.

Hyde-Lay wasn't the only teacher helping, either. After Steve and Jamie enrolled at SMUS in early December, a group of teachers at the private school began giving up some of their free time to tutor the newcomers and bring them up to speed. Steve quickly discovered that the school's teachers expected work to be completed and turned in promptly. And as the year wore on, as Steve realized that Hyde-Lay and the rest of the teachers at SMUS were investing their time and energy in improving his academic standing, he decided he should hold up his end of the bargain as well.

"Obviously, SMUS had a much higher emphasis academically. Students weren't to be left behind. We'd be pushed to keep up and to accept responsibility," Steve says now. "Also, Ian was instrumental in holding us accountable and providing preventative measures, too— he put a huge emphasis on that."

By the end of his Grade 11 year, Steve's marks had improved considerably. His first full report card from SMUS showed straight Bs. John and Jean Nash were ecstatic with the improvement, and Steve was proud of himself, too. It was clear the move to St. Michaels University School had been the right one.

As far as Steve is concerned, few if any events in his development as both a basketball player and a person were as important as his transfer to SMUS and the opportunity to learn from Ian Hyde-Lay. Their relationship remains strong to this day, with the NBA star and his high school coach exchanging regular e-mails and phone calls. Whenever Steve has undergone a challenging period during his post–high school career, he has invariably received an inspirational message from Hyde-Lay reminding him that "The cream rises to the top" or "Fortune favors the bold."

"I think the academics at SMUS were important, but even more so was the fact that I got to play for a terrific coach who taught me a lot, had a great eye for the game, a great understanding, and really saw things that other people didn't see—and that helped me a ton," Steve says now.

"He also was really good at seeing my game and breaking it down, to: 'This is what you could be really good at, this is what you could change'—you know, always giving me valuable advice that I don't think I would have got from many people."

Though there would be plenty of other helping hands for Steve during his career, Ian Hyde-Lay's were perhaps the most important, providing just the right mix of support and discipline at a time when the teenager needed it the most.

3

THEY ALL FALL DOWN

"It was like I was trapped in an elevator and I'm screaming, but nobody could hear me."
—Steve Nash, college scholarship hopeful, 1991–92

It had been a half-dozen years since Steve Nash had first formally laid out his plans, for all the world to see, in an elementary-school assignment entitled "Me."

He and his sixth-grade classmates had been asked by their teacher to outline a blueprint for their futures. Eleven-year-old Steve had written matter-of-factly that he would attend college on an athletic scholarship and one day become a professional athlete.

But now, in the late summer of 1991, as his all-important senior year of high school approached, that plan was in jeopardy. The athletic scholarship Steve had carefully aimed toward for at least six years remained a frustratingly elusive goal.

Despite playing for the British Columbia All-Star Team, and despite being considered a strong enough player to earn an invitation to training camp with Canada's senior national men's squad as a seventeen-year-old, Steve Nash had thus far been universally ignored by U.S. college recruiters.

Steve had watched American college players for countless hours on television and was confident he possessed both the skills and the athletic ability to compete against them. Steve and the B.C. All-Star Team had been invited to the prestigious Las Vegas prep tournament that summer, where he had seen and played against some of the finest U.S. high school prospects, including future NBA teammate Jason Kidd. Steve had acquitted himself well in that tournament but, sadly, few of the hordes of college coaches and scouts in attendance had bothered to check out the B.C. team's games. And later that summer, he had also played some exhibition games for the Canadian Junior National team, scoring 13 points off the bench in a game against Division 1 Long Beach State University, before becoming the final cut as the national squad trimmed its roster for the World Championships in Edmonton.

Still, not a single NCAA school had offered him a chance to play south of the border, even though many of the top high school players had been well known to scouts for years and were already committing to colleges while still in Grade 11.

It was disappointing, but not a complete shock. Steve had suspected that missing his entire Grade 11 high school season due to his transfer would severely limit his early exposure to U.S. college scouts, and unfortunately he had been right. Add in the fact that he was a skinny, white point guard from a little-known island off the west coast of Canada and it was understandable that college recruiters hadn't beaten down the door of his family's Greater Victoria home with offers in hand. At the time there were no NBA franchises in Canada and no players in the NBA who had emerged from Canadian schools, and the relatively few Canadians who were breaking through as contributing players in the NCAA were mainly seven-footers.

Steve was encountering an inherent prejudice built up in the American system, which at that time basically said that Canadians couldn't possibly fill a "skill" position such as point guard at the U.S. Division 1 college level. There was also the fact that Steve wasn't particularly tall, and the fact that he was white, and thus labeled by many, sight unseen, as "non-athletic." All this was understandable, perhaps, but endlessly frustrating when Steve fiercely believed he was good enough.

"It was like I was trapped in an elevator and I'm screaming, but nobody could hear me," Steve would describe the experience years later to *Sports Illustrated*.

As his senior year approached, Steve knew his window for catching the attention of the U.S. basketball world was small. He was determined, almost desperate, to do everything possible to make somebody take notice. So late in the summer, just a couple of weeks before classes at St. Michaels University School began, he paid coach and athletic director Ian Hyde-Lay an on-campus visit. Steve knew he needed a game plan, and his coach was the man he trusted to draw it up.

"Do you think I'm good enough?" he asked Hyde-Lay bluntly during the summer meeting. It was time to put everything on the line. He could only hope that his coach believed in his abilities as much as he did.

"There's no question you're good enough, Steve," Hyde-Lay responded.

"Will you help me to get there?"

"I'll do everything I possibly can," the coach promised. "But you've got to realize that with these big U.S. schools, they're already looking to sign the top high school players as they finish their Grade 11 seasons, or even earlier. You haven't even *had* a Grade 11 season."

Despite that sobering reminder, Ian Hyde-Lay was true to his word. As the 1991–92 school year began, he wrote on Steve's behalf to a cross-section of approximately fifty of the top college programs in the United States, including powerhouses Duke, Indiana, Virginia, and Utah. He wrote to all of the schools in the Pacific-10 Conference, the league geographically closest to Victoria, which included one of Steve's favorite college teams, the University of Washington Huskies, who were just a four-hour car and ferry trip away. "I believe Steve Nash is a great talent, a real diamond in the rough who has the potential to be a terrific Division 1 player," the SMUS coach wrote in those letters.

That barrage of mail resulted in a handful of responses, including letters from major basketball programs at Virginia, Indiana, Miami, Long Beach State, Clemson, and Utah. While most schools offered polite rejections, a few requested a videotape of Steve, which Hyde-Lay dutifully sent.

As the season progressed, Steve held up his part of the bargain by leading a dominant SMUS Blue Devils squad to the top of the B.C. high school rankings. Nevertheless, the early interest from U.S. colleges seemed to mysteriously dry up. By Christmas, not a single NCAA recruiter had come to watch Steve play in person. Even as Nash and the Blue Devils turned in an outstanding performance at the twenty-four-team Encore Invitational tournament over the holiday break in Tucson, Arizona, not one college could be bothered sending anybody to check out the Canadian point guard. For both Steve Nash and Ian Hyde-Lay, the silence from south of the border was disturbing.

Only one U.S. college seemed to have taken the initiative when it came to Steve. Santa Clara University, a private, four-thousand-student school located about forty-five minutes south of San Francisco, California, was not one of the schools that Hyde-Lay had contacted for Steve. Still, they had written to the SMUS coach asking for a videotape of his star player. Hyde-Lay was only too happy to oblige.

After practically having to beg other schools to consider him, Steve was pleased to hear about the unsolicited interest. He didn't know anything about Santa Clara, but at least they seemed to know something about him.

Veteran basketball coach Dick Davey was walking toward his office on the upper level of Santa Clara's Toso Pavilion when he heard giggling coming from down the hallway.

Sticking his head inside an office door, Davey discovered junior assistant Scott Gradin locked in on the television set in front of him. Gradin was busy rewinding and replaying one section of a videotape over and over again.

Davey, then in his fifteenth season as an assistant coach with the Broncos, asked Gradin what was so funny.

"You gotta look at this," the younger coach replied, motioning Davey to check out the action on the screen. "This guy makes people fall down."

It was mid-December, well into the NCAA basketball season, and as the lead assistant for the Broncos, Davey had far more pressing matters on his mind. But curiosity got the better of him and he stepped inside.

Davey waited as the assistant rewound the video to the right spot and pressed play. After watching the tape, he had to agree—the video was funny. It was grainy and shot in poor light from a lousy angle, but it clearly showed a slender, white guard in a blue-and-white uniform winding his way through a series of seemingly hapless high school opponents. On a few occasions, the boy's dribble moves, footwork, and head-fakes were so good they indeed were making his defenders fall over simply trying to stay with him.

The player featured in this video was a little-known Canadian point guard whom Santa Clara had been tipped off to by a coaching contact months earlier. Santa Clara head coach Carroll Williams had asked his staff to request some video from the prospect's high school in Victoria, British Columbia.

It was impossible to determine by watching the tape exactly how good this kid was. Dick Davey didn't think the level of competition the boy was obviously dominating was particularly high, and the quality of the video was far from the best. Still, this Steve Nash was worth a second look. That much was obvious.

Scott Gradin, twenty-five and in his first NCAA coaching job, spent most of his time on recruiting chores for Santa Clara, which, because of its size, can't typically compete with the big-budget college basketball programs across the United States when it comes to attracting blue-chip high school players. It was Gradin's job to pursue prep prospects such as Nash, to check them out and make the contact with them permitted under the NCAA's strict recruiting rules.

Before leaving the office where Gradin was working, Davey asked him to request another video from the small, private Vancouver Island high school where Steve Nash was in the midst of his senior season. Gradin was pleased to hear that Davey was at least interested in giving the kid another look. He continued to examine the videotape, stopping it, rewinding it, and even watching it in slow motion. Sure, the tape wasn't the greatest quality, and even Gradin was uncertain about the level of competition, but there was no denying this young man's skills. His dribbling and footwork were so precise that the ball seemed to move along as an extension of his body, and no matter what move he made, the boy never had to look down at the ball. As he continued to study the video, Scott Gradin was already thinking: *We've gotta get this kid.*

While Ian Hyde-Lay did his best to showcase Steve to U.S. colleges, the talented teenager was leading a powerful SMUS team to the kind of dominating season rarely, if ever, seen before in B.C. high school basketball.

Paired with Milan Uzelac, a member of the previous year's SMUS team and Nash's backcourt teammate from the B.C. Under-17 All-Star Team, Nash was unstoppable at point guard, recording nearly a triple-double—hitting double figures in three statistical categories—per game. For his Grade 12 season, Steve would average 21.3 points, 11.2 assists, and 9.1 rebounds, easily one of the finest campaigns in B.C. high school history.

More importantly, however, with Nash at the controls, the Blue Devils had become one of the most dominant teams ever. They would finish the season with a 50–4 record, but this SMUS juggernaut never lost a game while playing at full strength. Only once did the team lose with Steve in the lineup—a 7-point defeat at the hands of Austin Lathrop High School of Fairbanks, Alaska, in the semifinal of the Tucson holiday tournament. That game, in which two other SMUS starters sat out with injuries, would be the only time during Steve's one-season high school career that he personally tasted defeat.

The biggest challenge for Nash and the Blue Devils that season came from close to home. Both the Alberni Armada, from the central Vancouver Island mill town of Port Alberni, and the crosstown Greater Victoria rival Belmont Braves had more height and, along with it, plenty of skill of their own. At one time during the season, the three teams were ranked one-two-three in the province, and games between the Island rivals drew huge crowds. In fact, the final of the SMUS Invitational Tournament between SMUS and Belmont attracted enough interest to be moved into the University of Victoria's 2,500-seat McKinnon Gym.

Belmont was one of the four teams to beat SMUS that season, but the Braves turned the trick while Steve Nash was sidelined with a partially separated shoulder. The Blue Devils' other two losses came against Harry Ainlay High School of Edmonton and fellow private school Vancouver College, although both Nash and Miller were injured for those games as well.

At full strength, this SMUS team was intimidating. It didn't have an abundance of height—not a single player was taller than six-foot-four—but it had tremendous depth, and it played suffocating defense, which fueled a deadly fast-break led by Nash's peerless passing. It also boasted three B.C. Under-17 Team players in Steve Nash, Jamie Miller, and Milan Uzelac. Among the deep bench for SMUS was Steve's younger brother Martin, a supremely talented guard in his own right who would go on to post six 50-plus-point games as a senior for SMUS the following season, and good friends Chris Isherwood, Damian Grant, and Brent McLay.

Ian Hyde-Lay used this talent to full advantage, drilling his players in fundamentals and making sure they employed their bulk, toughness, and discipline to dominate the boards on most occasions. The Blue Devils played with a rare confidence that allowed them to impose their will on opponents nearly every night.

Leading the way was their point guard, who was certainly making the most of his only high school season.

But even as Steve put together a dream campaign, interest from the U.S. colleges remained minimal. One by one, the larger schools that had expressed initial interest in him had stopped calling or writing. Even the schools that had promised to scout him in person failed to come through. The basketball office at Virginia told Ian Hyde-Lay that it was planning to send somebody to the Vancouver Island Championship tournament in Nanaimo to evaluate Steve. This was the tournament that would determine which teams would move on to the provincial championships. But nobody showed up. Initial interest from Indiana and Long Beach State also waned. As he progressed through one of the best seasons ever compiled by a B.C. basketball player, Steve wondered exactly what he had to do to attract some attention.

The one school that expressed unflagging interest in Steve as his senior season marched toward a conclusion was Santa Clara. While the larger programs fell silent, Scott Gradin was constantly on the phone with the Victoria youngster and his family, keeping in touch and letting him know that the Broncos wanted him. Steve still didn't know much about Santa Clara, however, and it seemed some of their coaching staff didn't know much about Canada, either.

"This past summer I was in Santa Barbara [California] and this great kid from Canada was playing there," Dick Davey said to Steve in one of the Santa Clara coaching staff's numerous recruiting calls. "I can't remember his name but he's from Montreal ... Is he in your league?"

Nevertheless, Steve enjoyed the conversations with Davey and fellow assistants Larry Hauser and Scott Gradin. They also provided him with a security blanket. While it was frustrating that the bigger colleges weren't more interested, at least the Broncos were still calling.

Canadian schools were also interested in Steve, especially those in British Columbia, including his hometown UVic Vikes. But with his sights set on making the NBA, Steve didn't consider staying in Canada a serious option. Only Simon Fraser University in Burnaby remotely interested him, because, at that point, it played in the smaller U.S. National Association of Intercollegiate Athletics and at least faced American competition on a regular basis. But Simon Fraser's head coach, Jay Triano, who had himself been selected by the Los Angeles Lakers in the eighth round of the 1981 NBA draft, told Steve, "If your goal is to make the NBA, then go to the States."

Santa Clara University certainly wasn't the sort of major U.S. basketball program Steve had been hoping to end up at, however. In fact, his teammate and best friend Jamie Miller had taken to referring to it as "Santa Claus State." But as he talked more with Scott Gradin and the other Santa Clara coaches, Steve learned a few things about the school. The Broncos weren't a big-name program, but they had produced Los Angeles Lakers forward Kurt Rambis, an NBA player Steve had actually heard of. They also typically played some of the powerhouse Division 1 schools as part of their annual non-conference schedule. For the second game of their upcoming season, for instance, the Broncos would face UCLA in the Bruins' fabled Pauley Pavilion. Steve's friends might be making fun of Santa Clara, but the Broncos weren't complete NCAA lightweights, he was discovering.

As the Blue Devils' regular season ended in early March, only Santa Clara was still in regular contact with Steve. It was disappointing that, despite a tremendous season in which he had done everything expected of him and more, there wasn't more interest from the United States. *It's unlucky,* Ian Hyde-Lay thought to himself as the season concluded. *But for a six-foot-one white kid from Canada, that's probably just the way it is.*

All Steve could do was continue to play hard and hope that he could turn more heads. And despite the considerable competition locally, Nash and the Blue Devils rolled through the Vancouver Island tournament, winning their first two games by 77- and 49-point margins. In the Island final, Steve poured in 28 points to lead the Blue Devils to an 80–71 win over Alberni in what would be their closest game of the provincial playoffs.

The victory sent the Blue Devils into the B.C. Senior AAA Boys' Basketball Championship tournament, by far the premier event on the province's high school sports calendar. For this historic mid-March tournament, the high school game is taken out of the small school gyms and moved into the Pacific National Exhibition Agrodome, where wide-eyed players can suddenly find themselves performing in front of crowds in the thousands.

Every player in British Columbia dreams about getting to this event, and Steve Nash was no different. He had ridden the bench the previous March, watching SMUS finish eighth in the tournament, but this time would be much more exciting. This was his chance to make a mark on the forty-seven-year history of the event.

Expectations for the Blue Devils and Steve Nash were huge as they opened the tournament with a 101–46 win over the overmatched Columneetza Cougars from Williams Lake, a small town in the rugged interior of British Columbia. It was hardly a test for Nash or his team, but it would turn out to be an extremely important game in the young point guard's career.

4

VICTORIA'S SECRET

"You know, I never really lost the belief that something would arise. I just thought: 'Hang in there and you'll get an opportunity.' And I did."

—Steve Nash, Santa Clara recruit, April 1992

Santa Clara assistant coach Dick Davey arrived in the Agrodome well before the Blue Devils' first B.C. tournament game. By the time SMUS took to the floor for the warm-up, he was seated several rows up in a mainly empty section of the aging arena.

Davey had flown up to Vancouver from Portland, where the Broncos had been eliminated from the post-season West Coast Conference tournament. The veteran NCAA coach was in the Agrodome for one reason—to check out the point guard prospect whom junior assistant Scott Gradin had for weeks now been enthusiastically promoting to anybody on the Santa Clara coaching staff who would listen.

Several weeks after Broncos coaches had watched the first video of Steve Nash, a second tape had arrived in the mail at the Santa Clara basketball offices. Davey and Scott Gradin had screened it and found the quality of competition the young guard was playing against far better this time. Watching this tape, Davey thought Steve Nash resembled a younger version of Bobby Hurley, the All-American guard at Duke University. *Oh boy,* Davey told himself. *This kid's pretty good.*

Now Davey had been dispatched by head coach Carroll Williams to Vancouver for this recruiting visit. The Broncos were looking for a point guard prospect capable of eventually replacing John Woolery, a tough guard from Los Angeles who would be entering his junior NCAA season that coming fall. As he took his seat in the Agrodome, Davey wasn't sure if Steve Nash could be that player or not.

It didn't take Davey long to make up his mind. In fact, the game hadn't even begun by the time the coach had decided this kid had skills that were well beyond the average high-schooler, Canadian or American. His seamless ball-handling and passing and pure shooting stroke in warm-ups were proof enough for Davey that Nash had spent hours in the gym, and, seeing him in person, it was easy to tell the boy had enough size and quickness to be an impact player in the West Coast Conference. Minutes after tip-off, Dick Davey had decided Scott Gradin was right. The kid on that funny videotape could play.

Davey surveyed the stands of the Agrodome for this afternoon, first-round game, which had typically drawn a sparse crowd. He looked over his shoulder and strained his eyes to peer across the dimly lit arena, searching for familiar faces. He could only hope that no other U.S. schools were on the trail of this kid. Steve Nash was a real find.

A reporter from the Victoria *Times Colonist*, who had noticed the coach in the stands, asked Davey what he thought of Nash. "We're highly interested in him," Davey replied. "He handles the ball better than any U.S. high school player I've seen this year. We would love to have him. We would sign him yesterday if he said yes."

After the opening-round game, Davey introduced himself to Steve, and he later spoke briefly with John and Jean Nash as well. He and Steve went out to a Chinese food restaurant across the street from the Agrodome for a soft drink. The boy came across as friendly and mature, with a good head on his shoulders, and his parents seemed like nice people too, Davey thought. He still hadn't noticed any other U.S. coaches hanging around. So far, so good.

Back at his hotel room, Davey phoned Santa Clara head coach Carroll Williams. "I'm going to stay up here for another day," he said. "This kid is really good."

The next day, Davey watched Steve Nash play one more game, an 85–74 second-round decision over the defending provincial champion Richmond Colts. The Colts were a much better test for SMUS, and Steve responded to the challenge, scoring 26 points and adding 7 assists and 10 rebounds in the win.

Dick Davey departed for Santa Clara after that game, secure in the knowledge that Nash was a blue-chip prospect who had, so far at least, escaped the net of other U.S. college recruiters. He could only hope that Victoria's Secret would remain under the radar for the next few weeks.

In B.C. high school basketball circles, meanwhile, Steve Nash was quickly cementing his place in history. The next night, while 3,500 fans watched in the Agrodome, he and the Blue Devils cruised to a 94–57 victory over the tartan-clad West Vancouver Highlanders, moving them into the Saturday night championship game. Steve had 16 points, 9 assists, 9 rebounds, and 7 steals, and the tenacious SMUS defense held eighth-ranked West Vancouver scoreless for more than ten minutes during the first half.

More than 4,200 fans rolled into the Agrodome for the next night's final, nearly filling the steamy agricultural exhibition arena to capacity. Steve and the Blue Devils were ready for prime time, too, shaking off a nervous first quarter to outscore the Pitt Meadows Marauders 20–0 over a seven-and-a-half-minute span early in the second half. Steve finished his final high school game with 31 points, 11 rebounds, 8 assists, and 4 steals as the Blue Devils beat the Marauders 76–48 in the biggest championship-game blowout in the tournament's history.

Following the final buzzer, Steve Nash was named the Most Valuable Player of the tournament after averaging

23.5 points and 7.5 assists over four games. But both he and coach Ian Hyde-Lay were quick to point out that it had been a true team effort, as the Blue Devils had outscored their opponents by an average 33 points in the tournament.

"It's going to be a long time before this school sees a collection of athletes together like this again," Hyde-Lay told a reporter on the floor of the Agrodome. "There's been a lot of focus on Steve Nash this year, but I think we had absolutely phenomenal seasons from a lot of other guys, too. We talk a lot about basketball being a team sport. I think these guys are a team in the truest sense, in that they have all put the team ahead of themselves."

Just how fine a collection of athletes the Blue Devils were became even clearer ten weeks later at the University of British Columbia, when many of the same boys powered SMUS to the B.C. AAA High School Rugby championship. Despite being relatively new to the game, Steve Nash was one of the outstanding players on the SMUS side, scoring 17 points in the provincial championship game on a try, 3 penalties, and a pair of converts.

Before turning his attention to rugby, however, Steve had some important business to take care of on the basketball front. Despite his tremendous season and MVP turn at the B.C. tournament in the Agrodome, Santa Clara was the only U.S. Division 1 college still showing serious interest in him. So, one month after his team had captured the provincial basketball championship, Steve departed on his official forty-eight-hour recruiting visit to the California school.

Steve arrived at Santa Clara on a warm, sunny day. He immediately felt as though he belonged on the Spanish-style campus with its wide sidewalks lined with palm trees and its appealing mission-style architecture. He thought Toso Pavilion, the bubble-domed gym where the Broncos played their home games, was on the small side for a Division 1 school, but at the same time he liked the feel of the court.

Steve bunked at an off-campus house with sophomore Santa Clara forward Pete Eisenrich, playing pool at the Benson Student Center and meeting many of his future teammates. The highlight of the weekend came on the basketball court, where he got a chance to run with future backcourt mates John Woolery and DeWayne Lewis, a pair of speedy guards from Los Angeles. *Geez, I don't get to play against guys this good all the time,* Steve thought to himself.

Scott Gradin, the assistant coach who had sold the rest of the Broncos' staff on the value of Steve Nash, was delighted to meet his prime prospect face to face during the visit. He was also amazed to see that several Broncos players naturally gravitated toward the Canadian. Gradin's instincts had been right—besides being a terrific basketball talent, this kid had some innate charisma and leadership qualities. As Steve's recruiting visit neared its end, Gradin took him for a drive around the area. "I see a good marriage here between Santa Clara and Steve Nash," he said.

Steve felt the same way. By the time his return flight touched down in Victoria, he had already decided that he would commit to playing for the Broncos. Santa Clara wasn't the kind of major program he had hoped for, but it was the NCAA, and it was a foot in the doorway to his dreams.

Six days into the NCAA's spring signing period, Steve officially committed by signing a letter of intent to play at Santa Clara. Even with that commitment in hand, Broncos head coach Carroll Williams made his own trip to Victoria just days afterward. Williams wanted to meet the Nash family and answer any questions they might have about the basketball program and his school. Jean Nash made dinner and Williams showed the family a video about the university. He also informed the family that in his twenty-two years as head coach all but three Broncos players had earned degrees, something in which John and Jean took great comfort. Later in the evening, Ian Hyde-Lay popped by to meet Steve's future coach.

While Williams's visit made the Nashes feel better about the fact that their eldest son would soon be leaving home to attend school and play basketball in another country, it also convinced the veteran coach that the Broncos had recruited a gem. Williams had already been impressed with Steve's skills on the court and the young man's personality. But now he was also taken by the warm atmosphere in the Nash home.

John and Jean Nash had moved from South Africa to Canada when Steve was eighteen months old, so that their children would not have to grow up in the shadow of apartheid. They were the kind of parents who put their kids first, and all three children had turned out well. Martin Nash, less than two years younger than Steve, was an outstanding soccer and basketball player in his own right, but Williams could detect no jealousy in the quiet eleventh-grader, who seemed genuinely excited for his more outgoing big brother and the opportunity he was about to embark upon at Santa Clara. Kid sister Joann, a multi-sport junior high athletic star herself, was already a confident, intelligent young woman who frequently joined in the conversation during Williams's visit and obviously loved her brothers. Father John Nash's enthusiasm and friendliness was infectious, and mother Jean had clearly been a major source of Steve's determination, work ethic, and sense of loyalty. Steve Nash obviously had a highly supportive and loving family. As Williams drove back to his hotel, the veteran coach thought: *He comes from good stock.*

The story of how a future NBA MVP got the collective cold shoulder from the big college recruiters would grow into a near-legend over the ensuing years, and coaches from a number of major U.S. college programs were put on the hot seat to explain why they didn't bother to check out the Canadian kid.

Looking back on it now, Steve isn't all that surprised at the lack of interest. Canadian prospects in the early 1990s simply didn't get that close a look from many U.S. schools, unless they happened to be seven-footers.

Years later, Pepperdine University coach Tom Asbury would sum up the scenario for the *Los Angeles Times*. "When you're at Pepperdine, you get, oh, three hundred letters a year [from players looking for scholarships]. And for a white guard from Canada you're probably not going to do a lot of follow-up."

Since that time, basketball has been effectively globalized, and it's doubtful another prospect such as Steve would go nearly unnoticed, whether he played in Canada or Cameroon.

"I think lots of coaches just weren't sold on me," Steve says now. "You know, they're seeing a small white guy, they're thinking: 'He's not athletic enough.'

"Someone once told me that [college coaches] didn't necessarily believe what they saw. They said: 'Hey, this guy's really good.' But they just didn't believe it. They had a hard time convincing themselves that it was real."

Although at the time it was disappointing not to receive more interest from bigger schools, Steve was always confident he would find a way to get where he wanted to go.

"I never really lost the belief that something would arise," he says. "I just thought: 'Hang in there and you'll get an opportunity.' And I did.

"I was just fired up that I was going to get a chance at Santa Clara. It was great for me. You know, I had wanted to go to UCLA or Washington or Georgetown or Syracuse, or wherever. But in the end I was just happy that I was going to get a chance to play against those teams…. It worked out perfect."

As he wrapped up his high school days at St. Michaels University School in June 1992, Steve had accomplished his goals. He had won a U.S. college basketball scholarship and he had achieved the grades necessary to get into university. He had also made an impression on his classmates, judging by his senior entry in the 1991–92 SMUS yearbook:

"Stephen came to SMUS just after school started in Grade 11, making headlines everywhere. This star basketball player is also a stud off the courts gaining attention from many female followers…. Steve will have opportunities next year that will enable him to expand his athletic horizons and will likely be seen in the NBA one day."

5

GROWING PAINS

"I started the year and I was questioning whether I should even be playing the game ..."
—Steve Nash, Santa Clara freshman, 1992–93

He opened his eyes, glanced around the sparse dormitory room with its matching bunks and twin desks, and slowly squeezed them shut again. Steve Nash didn't want to wake up—not if it meant facing another day like those he had experienced for the past couple of weeks.

He was homesick. He missed his mom and dad, his younger brother Martin and kid sister Joann. He missed the family's tiny white dog, Quincy. He missed Victoria and all of his friends back home.

Steve's big dreams of college basketball stardom at Santa Clara University had morphed into a recurring nightmare. It was mid-November 1992, and he found himself in a situation he had never before experienced in the five years since he'd seriously taken up the game. For the first time, the eighteen-year-old had begun to doubt that he had what it takes to reach the sport's highest level.

Less than three months earlier, Steve had packed up his things, said goodbye to his family and friends, and made his way to the Bay Area college, excited about the chance to play basketball at the NCAA level and go to school in California. Things had gone pretty well for Steve at first, too, as he'd settled into his Santa Clara dorm with roommate and fellow freshman Jake Sedlock, an easygoing, six-foot-seven forward from Klamath Falls, Oregon, who was also a rookie in the Broncos basketball program.

During early-season workouts and scrimmages, Steve had held his own against decidedly tougher competition than he had faced in high school, and he had even dominated a few of the sessions. But during the last couple of weeks he had come down with a severe case of the flu and become so dehydrated that he'd had to be hospitalized for one night and placed on an IV.

The sickness had worn Steve down, and he had probably returned to practice at least a day too soon. Now he was finding himself unable to compete against the bigger, stronger Santa Clara backcourt players, particularly junior John Woolery, the Broncos' starting point guard.

During the past two weeks, Woolery had completely dominated Steve during practice sessions, muscling him off the basketball and stealing it from him seemingly at will. Steve found his own confidence level dipping to all-time lows. For the first time since junior high, he questioned whether he was good enough even to play at the Division 1 college level, never mind the NBA.

Making matters worse was the fact that coach Dick Davey seemed to be especially hard on him during these pre-season practices. Over the summer, the man who had recruited Steve at the B.C. high school tournament in the Agrodome had become the Santa Clara head coach, taking over from Carroll Williams, who was now the university's athletic director. Steve thought Davey had changed. The friendly man who had welcomed him into the Broncos' fold in March was now a demanding head coach who definitely wasn't shy about letting his players know when they had made mistakes. Certainly a freshman named Steve Nash felt himself on the sharp end of Davey's verbal barbs as he struggled through the long November practice sessions.

John Woolery had been all Steve could handle even before he got sick. Now the veteran guard was simply overpowering his young teammate, continually picking the ball cleanly from Steve during practices, tipping away his passes, and generally making him look like a junior high point guard. Steve had long prided himself on his ball-handling above all else. It was humiliating to have a guard who wasn't even all-conference stealing it from him time after time.

"Hydes, I can't get the ball up the court against this guy," Steve wrote his former high school coach in an e-mail. "I can't get it over center against Woolery in practice."

"Stick with it," Ian Hyde-Lay wrote back. "Just keep knuckling down, things will always turn in your favor."

What Steve didn't realize was that John Woolery was much better than outsiders gave him credit for. He had emerged out of the powerhouse program at Fairfax High School in Los Angeles that had produced NBA players Sean Higgins and Chris Mills. He wasn't a great shooter, but he was hard-working, smart, cat-quick, long-limbed, and one of the best defensive players in the West Coast Conference. While Steve fretted over the fact that Woolery was giving him fits on the practice floor, his older Santa Clara teammates didn't think twice about it. They knew from their own experience that John Woolery was a terrific defender. It was only natural he'd give a raw freshman from Canada a few problems while showing him the ropes.

Coach Dick Davey, though, was mildly surprised to see his prize recruit struggling through early November. Every time Steve failed a task in practice, every time he turned the ball over or made a bad pass or looked like he was in over his head, Dick Davey was disappointed. And he didn't hesitate to let the rookie know how he felt, either. He had expected Steve Nash to jump in and be an immediate contributor to the Santa Clara program. In fact, he already believed that Nash had the potential to play beyond the college level, and the coach felt it was his duty to bring out that potential using whatever means necessary. Davey believed he had a responsibility to be tough on all his players in practice. That way, he reasoned, they would be all the more tough when it came to real games.

But as Nash floundered, Davey began to harbor tiny doubts about whether he might have misjudged this Canadian kid. Had he overrated Steve? He didn't think so, but so far the freshman wasn't living up to his promise.

John Woolery, meanwhile, also believed that the tougher he was on Steve Nash, the better the kid was going to be in the long run. He had been impressed with the newcomer during Steve's recruiting visit to Santa Clara the previous spring, and he was again impressed with Nash's obvious desire to improve. Steve constantly asked questions of Woolery, and if the veteran made a suggestion, he returned a couple of days later with the advice already put to good use. Despite Steve's clear frustration at being schooled by his elders, Woolery noticed that the kid was often in Toso Pavilion before and after practice working on his game alone. Sometimes Steve was on the gym floor late into the night. *He works harder than anybody I've ever played with, by far,* Woolery thought to himself early in Nash's freshman campaign.

Santa Clara assistant coach Scott Gradin also remained confident in his prize recruit, and as that freshman fall unfolded, Gradin kept a protective eye on the young man. Gradin wasn't too concerned about Steve's performance in practices. He could clearly see the Canadian was frustrated, but he knew this was part of the process that nearly every college freshman has to go through. It was a major step up from high school to college ball. The play was faster, much more physical, and it was also now a business rather than simply a game. The fact that Steve was far from home just added to the challenge. There were bound to be some hard lessons and bumps along the way.

While the Broncos' new head coach regularly unleashed a lot of harsh criticism when he was disappointed with Steve's performance, Scott Gradin was always nearby to provide Nash with a pep talk or a comforting arm on his shoulder to help soothe the sting. Steve was grateful to have Gradin around at a time when there wasn't much that looked positive or gave him cause to feel confident or hopeful about his basketball career.

But the bottom line through these dark days was that basketball just wasn't fun any more. Steve found himself dreading practice for the first time in his life. Everything he did seemed to disappoint his new coach. The provincial title he had won at SMUS, all the good things he had done as a B.C. high school basketball star seemed light-years away. As Steve pulled himself out of bed on yet another November morning at Santa Clara, he wanted nothing more than to pack up everything and go home.

Something deep inside wouldn't let him do that, though. How could he go back to Victoria after less than three months and admit that he hadn't been able to cut it in U.S. college basketball? How could he give up so quickly on his long-held dreams of making a career for himself in the game? How could he let Dick Davey get the best of him? Steve threw on his clothes and headed to his first class of the day. Things at Santa Clara had to get better sometime soon … didn't they?

Despite all the pre-season difficulties at Santa Clara, Steve found himself growing excited as his first NCAA season tipped off. He scored his first basket—his only points—

as the Broncos beat San Jose State on the road to open their 1992–93 campaign. A few days later, he got a chance to play in historic Pauley Pavilion, the gym that had spawned ten NCAA-champion UCLA Bruins teams under legendary coach John Wooden. But coming off the bench in this game, Steve was nervous, and it showed. He missed three easy shots—a couple of them badly—and turned over the ball twice before being yanked from the game by Dick Davey. As he returned to the bench for good in what would be a 69–60 Santa Clara loss, Steve was upset over his performance.

Scott Gradin slid down the bench and offered a few words to the freshman. "Three years from now, the difference will be that you'll be 3-for-3 with 3 assists during that same stretch," the assistant coach quietly reassured him.

The pep talk helped comfort Steve, who was placing tremendous expectations on himself and agonizing whenever he didn't meet them. He wanted to believe that Gradin was right, that he would learn and improve and develop into a valuable player for Santa Clara. Getting there was going to be even tougher than he had expected, though.

Steve Nash's big chance to break into the Broncos' lineup as a contributing regular came just eight games into the season, when John Woolery injured his left knee and had to undergo arthroscopic surgery. Woolery would be forced to miss three games. And despite Steve's obvious struggles with college-level play, Dick Davey decided to start the freshman in Woolery's place for all three contests.

Determined to put his shaky start at Santa Clara behind him, Steve pounced on this opportunity. In his first college start against the University of Minnesota Golden Gophers at Santa Clara's Toso Pavilion, Steve wowed the home crowd by scoring a team-high 15 points and hitting three of four three-pointers. Filling in for the injured Woolery at the point, he played twenty-seven minutes, ran the offense, and didn't turn the ball over once.

That game would prove to be Steve's breakthrough in a Santa Clara uniform. But he also played well in his two other starts during the Cable Car Classic tournament in Toso Pavilion. Sitting proudly in the stands for those games were his two high school coaches, Ian Hyde-Lay and Bill Greenwell. For Steve, it felt great to have them there, and to perform solidly in front of them.

After John Woolery's return to the Santa Clara lineup, Dick Davey decided he needed to find minutes immediately for the freshman, who was finally beginning to resemble the player he had recruited the previous spring. Davey moved Steve to the shooting guard position, where his three-point stroke evolved into a valuable weapon for the Broncos. Over the next eleven games, Steve averaged more than 11 points a contest from the two-guard spot, and also filled in at point whenever Woolery needed a breather.

With his early struggles behind him and his body now back at full strength, Steve's confidence began to soar. He averaged nearly thirty minutes a game during the final third of his freshman season, huge playing time for any first-year player. By the end of the schedule, he had scored in double-figures in a dozen games and hit a Santa Clara freshman-record 49 three-pointers. His 252 points was the highest season total for a Broncos rookie in fifteen years.

But while things were going well for Steve in games, he continued to feel the wrath of Dick Davey in practice. The head coach wasn't about to baby his freshman just because he had turned the corner and become a contributing member of the team. Instead, Davey seemed to push him even harder. He often yelled at Steve during practices and, during a road game at the University of San Francisco near the end of the regular season, he ripped into Nash at halftime for allowing his check to make passes into the post. Although Steve said nothing while the coach chewed him out in front of his team-mates in the locker room, Davey took his silence and the look on his face as a show of defiance. "If you don't like it," the coach yelled at a bewildered Nash, "you can take your ass back to Canada!"

But though Steve found Davey's harsh treatment confusing and troubling, what was happening on the court made up for it. With Steve now playing a major role, the Broncos had won six of their last seven games to surge into the post-season West Coast Conference Tournament at the University of San Francisco's Memorial Gymnasium.

When Santa Clara won its first two games of the sudden-death tournament, the team advanced to the final. And now there was a huge prize on the line. The winner of the West Coast Conference playoff tournament would receive an automatic berth into the prestigious NCAA Tournament, the event known as "March Madness" that Steve had watched on TV every year since he was a seventh-grader. Steve had dreamed of playing in the exciting, high-stakes NCAA Tournament for years. Now his team was just a single win away from doing that.

Nobody gave the Broncos much hope of capturing the NCAA berth, however. Standing in their way were the Pepperdine Waves, the top-ranked team in the conference. And when Pepperdine jumped out to a 19–5 lead in the first half, it seemed like Steve Nash's freshman year was coming to a close.

But something magical occurred in the second half of that game, televised live across the United States on ESPN. After recording just 3 points in the entire first half, Steve burst out of the locker room to score the first 8 points of the second, including two three-pointers. That sparked an amazing three-point assault by the underdog Broncos, who hit all nine long-range bombs they attempted during the final twenty minutes.

Steve finished the game nailing five of his six three-point attempts and scoring a career-high 23 points as Santa Clara stunned Pepperdine 73–63. More than four thousand fans went crazy over the underdog Broncos and their young hero. Supporters in the stands carried signs reading "We are NASH-TY" and hoisted the freshman onto their shoulders after the final buzzer.

Minutes later, the skinny Canadian became the first freshman ever to be named the WCC Tournament's Most

Valuable Player. As he stood there on the University of San Francisco floor, a certified college hoops hero, it was difficult for Steve to believe that, just months earlier, he had been tempted to give it all up and return home. *I started the year and I was questioning whether I should even be playing the game,* he thought to himself, *but I fought through it.*

Steve's shooting statistics over the final stretch of the season and the WCC Tournament were incredible. He had nailed fifteen of nineteen three-point attempts during the most crucial stage of the year. A star had been born in Santa Clara basketball.

"These are high-pressure games with a lot at stake," said former Los Angeles Lakers and UCLA great Kareem Abdul-Jabbar as a game analyst for ESPN, summing up the magnitude of Steve's performance. "For an eighteen-year-old freshman to be doing that well under this kind of pressure ... I think we're seeing something very unique."

Other observers felt the same way. In the wake of Santa Clara's upset win, *The San Francisco Examiner* ran a column with the headline: "Nash proves dreams do come true." The *San Jose Mercury News* offered up: "Freshman's story better than fiction."

"Everything I had hoped and dreamed for has come true," Steve told the *Mercury News* in a subsequent article. "Now I'll have to hope and dream for bigger things."

Those bigger things came in the form of the Broncos' first NCAA Tournament berth since 1987. Reaching the sixty-four-team college hoops extravaganza, which captures the interest of sports fans across North America for a full month every spring, was a major accomplishment for the surprising Broncos. In fact, one newspaper columnist from the area even wrote: "Santa Clara in the NCAA Tournament? Get serious."

But these Broncos weren't satisfied merely getting to the event known as the Big Dance; they wanted to cut a rug once they got there. Just one problem: their partner for the first round was mighty Arizona, the fifth seed overall, with a lineup including three future NBA players in Chris Mills, Khalid Reeves, and Damon Stoudamire, who would go on to win NBA Rookie of the Year honors with the Toronto Raptors in 1996.

The Wildcats, coached by white-haired master Lute Olson, had dominated the superior Pacific-10 Conference that season with a 17–1 record. Nobody was giving the Broncos, upset winners of the lightly regarded West Coast Conference, the slightest hope to win this game. They were the fifteenth seed out of sixteen teams in that region of the tournament, while Arizona was seeded number two. Up to that point in NCAA Tournament history, a number-fifteen seed had beaten a number-two seed only once in thirty-four tries.

While Dick Davey played up his team's underdog status to the media, he delivered a distinctly different message to the players in the locker room, as a crowd of 11,739 waited for the first-round game to begin in the Huntsman Center at Salt Lake City, Utah. "Outside this locker room, I don't think anybody out there thinks we can do it," he told his players. "But I know we can."

As Steve soaked up the words of his coach, they only intensified the excitement he was feeling about being in the NCAA Tournament. It was incredible to now be part of something he had always watched from the outside. The experience of coming out of the arena tunnel in his uniform with thousands of fans cheering, the TV cameras pointed at him and his teammates, and the bands playing sent chills down his back and raised goose-bumps on his arms. *This is college basketball,* he thought as the Broncos took the floor.

An inspired Santa Clara team charged out onto the court and grabbed a 12-point lead by the three-quarter mark of the first half. But the Wildcats began to assert their size and talent and scored 25 straight over the next ten minutes. With just over fifteen minutes left in the game, Arizona led 46–33 and the Cinderella Santa Clara team seemed destined for defeat.

But the upstart Broncos then fashioned what remains one of the greatest upsets in NCAA Tournament history, grabbing every loose ball and rebound for the rest of the game and taking advantage of Arizona foul trouble to regain the lead on a jumper by forward Pete Eisenrich with just two minutes and forty seconds remaining.

With the game on the line in the final minute, Arizona attempted to claw back by fouling Steve Nash and sending the freshman to the line. During the last thirty-one seconds, Steve made six straight free throws to seal the biggest victory in modern Santa Clara basketball history. Refusing to shrink under the intense pressure, Steve sprinted the length of the court to the foul line every time, eager to make each one of those free throws. The crowd in the Huntsman Centre, some of them waving "We Are NASH-TY" signs, went crazy as the Broncos mobbed each other on the shiny hardwood floor after the final buzzer in their 64–61 win had sounded.

"Obviously, there was a lot of pressure in that situation," Steve would later confide about the end of that game. "But if you want to be a basketball player at this level, those are the kind of moments you have to enjoy. All my life, I've wanted to be in that situation and I'm glad I didn't run from it."

Two days later, Santa Clara bowed out of the NCAA Tournament with a 68–57 loss to the tenacious Temple Owls of Philadelphia. But the Broncos and Steve Nash had certainly made their mark on the event. And along the way, Santa Clara coach Dick Davey was delighted to discover that his recruiting instincts had been right after all—that his prized freshman not only possessed major-college skills, he also had a knack for rising to the occasion when the pressure was greatest.

The breakthrough Steve Nash enjoyed at the college level in the spring of 1993 would carry on to international basketball that summer, first with Canada's Under-22 National team and later with the country's World University Games team. The player who two years earlier had been cut by the national junior team was easily selected in tryouts for these two elite summer squads. By now, Basketball Canada had identified Nash as a key component in its program. And Steve realized that playing for Canada represented a valuable chance to both improve as a player and pad his basketball resume.

With the Under-22 Nats, Steve got his first taste of just how challenging playing conditions can be in the international game. While facing host Argentina in an important contest that was part of a qualifying tournament for the following year's World Junior Championships, the young Canadian players found themselves pelted with ice (from the arena's concession stand), candy, and coins thrown by the home crowd. Steve was nailed in the back of the neck by an iceball that felt the size of a baseball. After a loss in what was a rough game, he and the Canadian team had to be escorted out of the stadium by police.

While that Canadian team narrowly failed to qualify for the world tournament, Steve and his teammates fared much better a month later at the World University Games in Buffalo. Despite being one of the youngest teams in the tournament, Canada advanced all the way to the gold-medal game against the heavily favored U.S. squad, which included one of Steve's future NBA teammates and best friends, Michael Finley, as well as Damon Stoudamire, who had suffered the huge upset loss to Steve and Santa Clara in the NCAA Tournament that spring.

Playing on home soil with a star-studded lineup of future pros, the United States was thought to be invincible in this tournament. But Nash and the Canadians threw a major scare into the Americans, taking a shocking

17-point lead to stun the nearly sold out Memorial Auditorium crowd and heading into the locker room at halftime up by a dozen points.

Although the upstart Canadians would eventually fall 95–90 to the Americans, Steve Nash turned plenty of heads in the performance with 11 points and an incredible 17 assists. If anybody in the U.S. college basketball world had missed his coming-out party with Santa Clara that spring, they certainly knew about the young Canadian now.

6

GREAT EXPECTATIONS

"It's sort of scary because it's do or die ..."
                    —Steve Nash, Santa Clara senior, 1995–96

At one end of the gleaming hardwood floor in the Lahaina Civic Center was a long table, running the length of the baseline. Each of the eighteen seats at that table was reserved for an NBA scout, player personnel director, or general manager. It was mid-November 1995, and these gentlemen weren't visiting tranquil Maui for sun and fun. They were in Hawaii to scope out some of college basketball's finest talent.

Steve Nash glanced at the table as he warmed up for the game he and his Santa Clara Broncos would tip off in just a few minutes. It was a huge contest, both for the Broncos and for his own career. As a highly rated senior in the early stages of his final college season, Steve was one of a handful of prospects these pro basketball bird-dogs were in Hawaii to check out.

Steve wasn't really surprised to learn that the list of NBA types assembled included Los Angeles Lakers executive Jerry West, Larry Riley of the Vancouver Grizzlies, and Gene Shue of the Philadelphia 76ers. The Maui Invitational pre-season tournament had attracted a strong eight-team field, including the nationally third-ranked Villanova Wildcats, the perennial powerhouse North Carolina Tar Heels, and the Michigan State Spartans. The event also included the defending NCAA Tournament champions, the mighty UCLA Bruins, whom Santa Clara would face in just a few minutes.

UCLA had several key players returning from the team that had captured the national championship the previous spring on the floor of the Seattle Kingdome. Currently ranked fourth in the NCAA pre-season polls, the Bruins were heavily favored against the Broncos, who were hoping to use this high-profile season-opener to make an early mark on the college scene.

The game also represented a huge opportunity for Steve Nash, because it would give him a chance to show what he could do as a senior against a top-flight opponent, something scouts were eager to see, since Santa Clara played the majority of its games in what was regarded by many as a second-tier conference.

Steve and his teammates believed that Santa Clara did not get nearly enough credit for being a good basketball team. It seemed people always considered them the underdogs, no matter how well they performed. In Steve's three previous seasons, the Broncos had gone to the NCAA Tournament twice. Although he had fleetingly considered transferring to a larger school that might have offered him more exposure, Steve decided after his sophomore year to stay on at Santa Clara. He had grown close to a group of teammates that included Jake Sedlock, Drew Zurek, Kevin Dunne, Lloyd Pierce, Marlon Garnett, Adam Anderson, and Phil Von Buchwaldt, a towering Frenchman who, since being recruited by Santa Clara, had learned much of his English by watching ESPN. Steve and head coach Dick Davey continued to clash through that second season, but the two eventually became more comfortable with one another, and both Nash and the team prospered as a result.

As a sophomore, Steve started all but three games and managed to average 14.6 points from the shooting guard spot to lead the Broncos in scoring. Following that season, playing with the Canadian senior national team, he went on to start every game, and the team finished seventh at the 1994 World Men's Basketball Championships in Toronto.

By far his most impressive campaign so far, though, was his junior year, when the Broncos ran up a sterling 21–6 record before losing to Mississippi State in the first round of the NCAA Tournament. During that season Steve moved into the starting point guard role, replacing the graduating John Woolery, and firmly cemented his status as a first-round NBA draft prospect. He averaged a career-best 20.9 points and 6.4 assists, tops in the West Coast Conference in both categories. He also finished among the top ten in the entire nation in four separate offensive statistical categories. All of this was enough to make Steve Nash the West Coast Conference's Player of the Year that spring.

It also placed Steve under a great deal of pressure. Now, with his senior season about to begin, the player who had practically been forced to beg for a scholarship just three years earlier was squarely in the sights of NBA scouts. He was grateful, but along with that status came huge expectations. This game against the UCLA Bruins was a chance for Steve Nash to open some more eyes in the NBA, but the flip side was the negative repercussions a poor performance could bring.

"It's sort of scary because it's do or die," Steve quietly admitted to a friend before the UCLA game that would begin his all-important senior season. "Things don't go your way, it could cost you millions of dollars ..."

It still seemed strange to Steve to think that many of these scouts would travel all this way to watch him, a player whom few college coaches had bothered to check out in person when he was in high school. This kind of attention might be business as usual for players such as Villanova's Kerry Kittles, North Carolina's Jeff McInnis, or UCLA's Toby Bailey, but it was certainly something new for him.

Steve now pushed all those distractions to the back of his mind and focused on the game ahead against the Bruins in the thick humidity of the Lahaina Civic Center, a 2,500-seat facility situated less than the length of a football field from the beach. As was typical for this popular pre-season event, the gym was completely sold-out for the Bruins-Broncos game, which was being televised live on ESPN back to the continental United States.

Despite the pressure on Steve to perform, the Santa Clara team was in the enviable position of being able to approach this game with a nothing-to-lose attitude. All the heat was on the defending national champs. "I can't believe a bunch of yahoos like us are about to beat UCLA," Steve joked with his teammates moments before taking the court.

As the game began, the highly athletic UCLA squad jumped and dunked its way out to an early 15–6 lead, looking as if it would run the smaller Santa Clara team right out of the sweaty gym. But the Broncos weathered the surge and settled in to make it a game. At halftime, Santa Clara held a surprising 38–36 lead, with Steve scoring 11 points despite foul trouble. In the second half, the senior point guard keyed an 11–0 run as the Broncos pulled away for a 78–69 victory over the stunned Bruins. The final box score clearly showed Steve's signature on the game: 19 points, 7 assists, and 2 steals. He had also held well-regarded UCLA point guard Cameron Dollar scoreless. Both Steve and the Broncos had faced a severe test to begin the season, and they had passed with flying colors.

"They just flat out beat us, there was no excuse," UCLA coach Jim Harrick said afterward. "They're a very experienced, talented, well-coached basketball team that's been in the NCAA Tournament two of the last three years. And they've got a terrific player in Steve Nash."

Many observers had similar thoughts two days later as the Maui Invitational came to a close. Santa Clara lost its second game of the tournament, falling 77–65 to the Villanova Wildcats of Philadelphia, but once again Steve posted solid numbers against a highly rated opponent with a 21-point, 6-assist, 6-rebound game. On day three of the event, Steve scored 23 more as Santa Clara beat Michigan State 77–71.

To make things even sweeter, Steve also got the chance in Maui to meet former Los Angeles Lakers great Magic Johnson and pose for a picture with the basketball legend. Through a mutual friend, Magic later signed his picture, inscribing it: "To Steve. Be cool and good luck. From Big Magic to Little Magic."

The performance in Hawaii was enough to vault tiny Santa Clara into the NCAA Top 25 rankings for the first time in twenty-three years. Meanwhile, Steve's profile, both with basketball insiders and with fans, was also soaring. Two weeks after his Maui experience, Steve was the subject of a five-page spread in *Sports Illustrated,* a magazine he had grown up reading. The story was titled: "Little Magic: Canadian export Steve Nash doesn't get much TV time at Santa Clara, but he might be the best point guard in the country."

While his name graced the pages of national sports magazines and his image made the nightly highlight reels on ESPN, Steve Nash in many ways lived the life of a typical college student during his senior year at Santa Clara.

He and five other friends—four of them Broncos basketball players—shared a rather ordinary three-bedroom bungalow located just off campus. It was nicknamed "The Fireplace" because it was right across Alviso Street from the Santa Clara Fire Station.

The house became a meeting place for Santa Clara basketball players and their friends. Its walls were decorated with basketball posters and banners from past NCAA Tournament games. Its kitchen was usually littered with delivery boxes from neighborhood pizza and chicken joints. And its television set showed a seemingly endless reel of sports highlights.

But while he attended classes and practice with his teammates and shared a messy, fun-filled house with a pack of roommates, a typical day for Steve Nash was also in many ways unlike that of the other Broncos. For an hour or two after every practice, he would dutifully head to the office of Santa Clara sports information director Jim Young to answer mail or do an interview that a newspaper or radio station somewhere had requested through the team. And when he returned home, there were usually messages waiting from more journalists or eager sports agents looking for the chance to represent him as a pro.

All the attention and hype that was building around him had been nice to begin with, but it was growing old quickly for Steve. It had also become a distraction, forcing him to be more disciplined in his scheduling so he could handle the increasing demands on his time. It was difficult to squeeze in enough sleep, eat properly, get to practice, and take care of his schoolwork in the final year of a Sociology degree.

When the Broncos took the court during his senior season, especially on the road, Steve found himself a marked man. Opposing fans tried their best to rattle him. "Canada sucks!" yelled one student during a game at Saint Mary's College in nearby Moraga, California. "You're going to the Clippers, Nash!" screamed another, referring to the then basement-dwelling NBA franchise in Los Angeles. By the end of that game, which the Broncos won, fans were chanting in unison—"C-B-A, C-B-A"—suggesting that Steve would be a better fit in the minor-league Continental Basketball Association than the NBA.

Steve's status as a potential draft pick also meant that he had to take precautions against injury in his senior season. He and his parents took out an insurance policy with American Specialty Underwriters in Kansas City that would pay him $1 million if a catastrophic injury ended his basketball career. If the game hadn't officially become a business for Steve Nash yet, it was certainly heading that way fast. He was still playing the sport he loved and having a lot of fun, but now there were huge stakes on the line each and every time he took to the court.

For both Steve and the Broncos, 1995–96 would prove to be an up-and-down campaign. Santa Clara was no longer the underdog that snuck up to bite unsuspecting opponents, especially after it had knocked off the mighty UCLA Bruins in Maui. That held true for Steve in particular, as teams were by now well aware of his capabilities and often designed their defenses specifically to take the ball out of his hands or to prevent him from getting good looks at the basket.

As a result, his scoring average fell significantly, from 20.9 points per game as a junior to 17 points in his senior season. His shooting percentage also dropped as he battled nagging thigh, hamstring, and foot injuries and struggled to find his offensive rhythm against defenses concentrated mainly on throwing him off his game.

"People look at the newspaper and they see me with 11 points, 9 points, 6 points, but they don't realize that other teams are doing the best they can to take me out of the game," Steve confided to a friend as the season wore on. "That's one thing I've had to come to grips with this year. But I'm getting used to that. It's a challenge and, hopefully, it'll make me a better player in the long run."

That senior season would be highlighted by some great games, including a 27-point effort on 10-for-13 shooting against the home-court University of San Francisco Dons, and a 24-point, 6-assist, 4-rebound night at Gonzaga University, which ended a seventeen-game home winning streak for the Bulldogs in Spokane.

Perhaps the most important contest that winter, however, came during the Christmas break, when Nash and the Broncos met Georgia Tech in the second round of Santa Clara's own Cable Car Classic in the San Jose Arena. Both teams had suffered disappointing defeats in the opening round of the tournament, but fans and scouts still looked forward to the matchup because it pitted New York schoolboy legend Stephon Marbury, a freshman at Georgia Tech, against Nash in a battle of NBA point guard prospects. The Georgia Tech star was being hailed as a once-in-a-generation talent, and speculation was already starting to mount that he would declare himself eligible for the NBA draft after just one season of college basketball. Going up against Marbury would be a terrific opportunity for Steve to win over the NBA evaluators who still had doubts about his quickness and athleticism.

While Marbury won the scoring battle between the two, racking up 22 points, he turned in only 4 assists. More importantly, the Tech team he was leading fell 71–66 to the Broncos. And while Steve scored only 9 points, he finished with 7 assists and was given the decision over Marbury by those paid to assess the game.

"Steve Nash won the battle of the point guards Saturday night," read the *San Jose Mercury News*.

"This wasn't a one-on-one game," Steve told the newspaper afterward. "If it was, I would have scored more points."

But for all the good moments in this crucial senior college season, frustration was frequently thrown into the mix. In mid-December, in front of thirteen NBA scouts at the Mecca in Milwaukee, Steve was held to just 6 field-goal attempts and 11 points in a loss to the Marquette Golden Eagles. In the opening round of the Cable Car Classic, he was limited to 6 points in a 70–49 loss to the Penn State Nittany Lions. In a 72–69 home-court defeat at the hands of the last-place Pepperdine Waves, he missed a seventeen-footer in the dying seconds that would have given the Broncos the lead. And in a late-season road trip, Steve scored just 8 points on 4-for-12 shooting in a key loss to the University of Portland Pilots.

"Mom, I'm sure the scouts are not interested in me any more after this," Steve told his mother in a somber phone call to Victoria following the Portland game. "But it doesn't matter. I'm still going to make the NBA."

Typical of the roller-coaster ride of his senior season, the huge victory that ended Gonzaga's home-court winning streak came just one game after that devastating loss in Portland. At Gonzaga, Steve rebounded nicely with 24 points, including a late jump shot and two free throws with one second left to ice a 77–71 win that clinched the Broncos a share of first place in the conference.

Just days later, that performance was likely on the minds of West Coast Conference coaches as, for the second straight year, they selected Steve Nash as the Most Valuable Player, making him only the eleventh player in conference history to win the award twice.

The Broncos would fall victim to an upset in the opening round of the WCC playoff tournament a week later at Toso Pavilion, however. Despite a 25-point effort by Steve on 7-of-10 shooting from three-point range, Santa Clara dropped a 63–60 stunner to the last-place Pepperdine Waves. It was a bitter moment for Steve as he realized that he had played his last game at Toso Pavilion, and possibly the final game of his entire college career. But immediately following the final buzzer, the exhausted senior walked to midcourt and pointed toward the fans in the stands. He raised his hands above his head and slowly clapped them together to salute the supporters who had been so generous to him through four years with the Broncos.

All that remained now for Santa Clara was to wait and see whether the NCAA Tournament selection committee would award them an "at large" berth in the event, as it had during Steve's junior season when the Broncos had also been eliminated in the first round of their conference tournament. The Broncos had recorded impressive wins over UCLA, Michigan State, and Georgia Tech during Steve's senior year, but they had also lost twice to Pepperdine, a school that didn't even register among the top two hundred in the NCAA. By no means was Santa Clara guaranteed a berth.

The entire team and friends gathered at The Fireplace to watch the Sunday selection show on CBS. And the room nearly exploded when the Broncos' name eventually appeared on the television screen as the sixty-first team in the sixty-four-team event. Santa Clara and Steve Nash were going to the Big Dance once again.

Steve entered his final NCAA Tournament on the limp, however. He was suffering from a sore left hamstring that had troubled him throughout his senior season. And as the Broncos approached their first-round game against the tenacious University of Maryland Terrapins in Arizona State University's Activity Center, coach Dick Davey was worried about the injury to his point guard.

Maryland boasted a tremendous defensive lineup, full of terrific athletes who loved to apply full-court pressure.

Davey was concerned how his team would break that pressure without their leader at 100 percent.

The Terrapins obviously weren't taking Nash lightly, either, injury or not. "We're well aware of Santa Clara, especially the guard Steve Nash," forward Keith Booth told reporters in somewhat tongue-in-cheek fashion. "We get ESPN on the East Coast as well."

The Terrapins wouldn't be keen on watching the highlights from this contest, however. As his final turn in the NCAA Tournament began, Steve delivered one of the finest performances of his Santa Clara career, scoring 28 points, adding 12 assists, 6 rebounds, and 2 steals. He also keyed a 14–0 Broncos run that broke open a close game in the second half and led to a convincing 91–79 Santa Clara win over Maryland. The headline in the following day's *San Jose Mercury News* read: "MONSTER NASH."

The Broncos were now just a win away from advancing to the following weekend's "Sweet 16" in Denver. This was as far as they had ever gone in the tournament during Steve's four years at the school, and with a veteran team that had bonded tremendously since the fall of 1992, he hoped they could all take that next step together.

Standing in the Broncos' way, however, were the Kansas Jayhawks, one of the premier programs in all of college basketball. This particular Kansas team boasted two future NBA players in forward Raef LaFrentz and point guard Jacque Vaughn. And on a day when Steve Nash would struggle mightily to find any success on his wounded leg, the Jayhawks proved to be far more than the Broncos could handle.

It was never really a game, as Steve missed all six of his shots in the first half and Santa Clara trailed 46–22 at the intermission. Nash didn't hit the scoresheet until making two free throws with less than fifteen minutes remaining in the game. His college career came to a disappointing end with a 1-for-11 shooting performance.

As he exited the court for the final time in a Santa Clara uniform with just over four minutes remaining, a fan who had yelled himself hoarse during the contest bellowed, "Thank you, Steve!" Thousands of Santa Clara fans felt the same way.

Nash refused to use his hamstring injury as an excuse for his performance. "I was fine," he said during the post-game press conference. "For the most part, I just didn't get it done.... I think the key was I just didn't make shots. I got some looks that I would normally knock down and I just didn't knock them down today. I think everybody's had one of those days. It's just disappointing that it had to be my last one."

It was difficult for Steve to come to grips with the fact his college career was over. But despite the disappointing ending, he was going out with his head held high. Over four years at the school, he had become the all-time assists leader in Santa Clara basketball with 510. He had also become the best free-throw and three-point shooter in Broncos history. For his senior year, during which he had endured the focus of every opponent's defensive game plan and the scrutiny of pro scouts, Steve had averaged 17 points, 6 assists, and nearly 4 rebounds.

While those numbers were solid, they were clearly inferior to what he had managed as a junior. Steve was aware that, despite what he had managed to accomplish over four years with a small NCAA basketball program, some people would look at that statistical slide and doubt his ability to succeed at the next level. And he was right, some people did just that.

A post-season column by Neil A. Campbell in *The Globe and Mail* quoted an anonymous NBA scout who summed up the sentiments of some of those doubters. "Steve Nash, he's taken as big a fall as anybody in the draft," the scout said. "Right now, he's maybe at the tail end of the first round, beginning of the second round."

The column explained that some NBA scouts were disappointed with how Steve had handled the pressure of his senior season. "It highlighted his lack of overall speed and quickness," the scout said. "He'd be in the bottom half of the [NBA] on the quickness scale."

Santa Clara head coach Dick Davey wasn't buying that assessment, however. Steve Nash had been a special player for the Broncos for four years, perhaps the greatest the school had ever seen. It was too bad that he had been injured for the conclusion of his senior season, but Davey was confident that he was going to be a solid NBA player. "There are a lot of doubters out there," the coach told *The Seattle Times*. "But I think he's going to be a tremendous pro or I'm not very smart. Someone is going to be very lucky."

Two weeks after Santa Clara was knocked out of the NCAA Tournament, Steve Nash won the U.S. college three-point shooting competition held at Fordham University in Manhattan in conjunction with the NCAA Final Four in New Jersey. Despite never having shot in such a competition before, he set the event record by scoring 22 of a possible 30 points in a semifinal.

But while that win helped put a more positive spin on the end of his college career, a difficult decision loomed for Steve as the Nike Desert Classic approached in Phoenix. He was among the top thirty-eight college seniors invited to the week-long camp run by the Suns and the NBA, an annual showcase in which players were divided into four teams and competed in a tournament format for the benefit of scouts and management.

The tournament was the perfect opportunity for Steve to convince critics once and for all that he was quick enough and athletic enough to be a starter in the NBA. There was just one problem, however. As the start of the camp grew closer, he was still plagued by the left hamstring injury that had slowed him during the NCAA Tournament and for much of his senior season.

Now Steve turned to Bill Duffy, the agent he had chosen to represent him as the NBA draft loomed. Duffy was a former Santa Clara player and someone Steve had already known and trusted for a couple of years. Going to

Phoenix was important for Steve's draft prospects, but he and Duffy also knew that attending the camp at less than full strength would be a tremendous risk. If he had a bad camp, his stock could fall considerably. Although draft forecasters had him pegged as a mid- to late-first-rounder, a poor camp could conceivably drop him into the uncertainty of the second round.

This was a difficult period for Steve. He had played basketball seriously since Grade 8 and now he felt as though all his work boiled down to a single opportunity. "If you have one bad week or game, all your hopes and dreams could go down the drain," he confided to a friend. "You've got to be ready."

Steve's hamstring certainly wasn't ready. But after mulling over the idea of skipping the Phoenix event altogether, he and Duffy decided that he would go. "I can possibly help myself there," Steve reasoned.

As it turned out, going to Phoenix was a wise decision. Steve managed to shrug off the hamstring problems to lead his Central team in impressive fashion over three games, averaging 8 assists, 7 points, and nearly 4 steals while showing he was a better defender against quick opponents than most scouts had given him credit for. The performance earned him a spot on the tournament's five-man All-Star Team and solidified his position as a first-round NBA pick. As draft day approached, it looked as though the gamble would pay off.

7

COME THIS FAR

"There were so many days growing up when I said to myself: 'There's no way I'm going back to the gym right now.' Then, two minutes later, I'd say: 'Yeah, you're going to the gym so that you can sit here on a day like this.'"

—Steve Nash, NBA draftee, June 26, 1996

Out of the corner of one eye, Steve Nash noticed the TNT cameraman scurrying toward his table. *The moment is finally here,* he thought to himself. *Finally.*

It was June 26, 1996, and Steve was seated at a circular banquet table in an area known as the Green Room, backstage at Continental Airlines Arena in East Rutherford, New Jersey. Sitting with him were his parents, his brother and sister, his aunt and cousin from England, his agent, Bill Duffy, and a few other close family friends.

Steve was among twenty players the National Basketball Association had identified as likely first-round picks in that evening's draft. They had all been invited to

New Jersey for a few days of dinners, parties, Broadway shows, and media interviews leading up to this night—when each of them would find out where he would begin his professional basketball career.

It was an impressive group, one that would eventually be counted among the strongest drafts in league history. Fellow point guards Allen Iverson of Georgetown and Stephon Marbury of Georgia Tech had declared themselves eligible as college underclassmen, and so had forward Shareef Abdur-Rahim of California. Connecticut junior Ray Allen was among the likely top picks, as was a high school hotshot from Philadelphia named Kobe Bryant.

The pre-draft buildup had been much longer than just this week for these players. For most of them, it had been years since they'd first been tabbed as NBA prospects. Since then, each had been waiting for this moment.

For Steve Nash, it had been a two- or three-year buildup, ever since the end of his sophomore season at Santa Clara, when talk about him having NBA potential had begun to circulate. His entire senior season with the Broncos had seemed heavily tied to the draft, with each game and, sometimes it seemed, each shot altering his position in the minds of NBA scouts. But the last six weeks leading up to this night had been a whirlwind of cities, hotels, restaurants, taxis, and gymnasiums as Steve had visited ten NBA teams for extensive pre-draft work-outs and interviews. The weeks immediately prior to every draft are consumed by such visits, as NBA teams attempt to scope out exhaustively all of the players they might conceivably want to select or trade for. Steve had visited Vancouver, Portland, Denver, Minneapolis, Indianapolis, Sacramento, Boston, Phoenix, Charlotte, and, finally, New York. It seemed like a blur.

During those visits, Steve had been subjected to all manner of evaluations, from measuring his wingspan, to charting his vertical leap, to seeing how he competed against other college players and journeyman pros. He had also been subject to psychological evaluations. In Portland, he was shown an ink pattern on a white page and told to use his imagination.

"Tell me what this is," said a Trail Blazers representative, holding up the paper.

Steve wasn't sure if this was supposed to be a joke or a serious exercise. But he wasn't surprised by the question. An NBA insider had already joked with him, "We've got to give you this psychological analysis to find out whether you're an ax-murderer or not. Of course, if you make 50 percent of your threes, we don't *care* if you're an ax-murderer."

While most of his visits had been low-key affairs, Steve's trip to Vancouver to audition for the Grizzlies had been anything but. There was huge media interest in his arrival, with reporters wondering whether the Grizzlies were planning to make a move to draft this unique, homegrown hoops hero. Vancouver was slated to pick at number three in the draft, considered too high a selection to use on Steve, but there had been plenty of speculation about a trade.

The New York Knicks had been Steve's final team visit, conducted in the two days before the draft festivities began. He and his family had been hosted by the team on the thirty-sixth floor of a chic downtown Manhattan hotel for two nights while he worked out in Westchester with the Knicks and spoke at one of the team's youth basketball camps. While Steve took care of business, his mother and sister took advantage of being in the Big Apple to shop Fifth Avenue and ride to the top of the Empire State Building. The Nashes were even able to watch brother Martin play with the visiting Vancouver 86ers against the New York Fever in an American Professional Soccer League game.

The family then moved across the Hudson River to East Rutherford, the site of the draft, where they were joined by a group of about twenty family members and friends who had made the trip east to share in Steve's big moment. For the next few days, they all enjoyed entertainment and meals arranged by the NBA and even managed to spot some celebrities, including Spike Lee, Gregory Hines, and Patrick Swayze.

Although he enjoyed the week immensely, Steve had begun to grow anxious by the time the big day finally arrived. He had agreed to spend the morning meeting with a modeling agency in Manhattan to be fitted for a new wardrobe. But when the car service returning him to New Jersey that afternoon got locked in tunnel traffic, Steve began to grow worried that he might miss his own party.

Fortunately, the driver delivered him back to the twenty-one-story Sheraton Meadowlands by mid-afternoon, just in time for Steve to watch a European

Cup soccer game on television in his hotel room with his cousin Lee and a gang of buddies from his college, high school, and junior high days. Hanging out with guys he had known all his life gave Steve the chance to unwind just a little as draft night approached.

After showering and changing into the loose-fitting black suit that had been sewn for him by an Atlanta tailor who specialized in making clothing for NBA players, Steve headed down to the lobby to catch the players' shuttle to the arena. Shortly after six o'clock the bus pulled out of the parking lot.

The players, each headed to the biggest moment of their lives to date, broke the tension by cracking jokes and talking. Steve nodded to Allen Iverson, who was projected by everybody to be the number-one pick that evening.

"You nervous?" he asked the Georgetown guard.

"No," Iverson replied. "No reason to be nervous now. Come this far."

The massive, white Continental Airlines Arena, home to the New Jersey Nets of the NBA and the New Jersey Devils of the National Hockey League, was just a five-minute shuttle ride from the hotel. Once inside, the draftees posed for a group photo with NBA commissioner David Stern. Then they were led into the Green Room, a private enclosure located behind the fifty-foot-high draft stage, a massive made-for-television set bearing the logos of all twenty-nine NBA franchises.

From that point, it was a waiting game for the players and their friends and families, who had been shuttled over on separate buses to join each of them at their table in the Green Room. As the draft's 7:30 p.m. start grew closer, the tension in the room increased. There was a lot on the line for everybody. Under the NBA's system, precisely where a player is selected has a direct bearing on his salary for the next three years. The number-one pick would receive more than US$3.2 million per season, while the final selection in the first round, the player who went twenty-ninth, would receive an average of about US$350,000 per year. For players who weren't picked in the first round, however, there were no guarantees. Teams did not even have to sign them if they chose not to.

It was widely expected that Steve would go somewhere in the mid to late first round, perhaps even a bit sooner than that. But there were no guarantees. While it was highly unlikely, it wasn't completely inconceivable that he would drop out of the first round altogether. What happened here in this arena during the next couple of hours would have monumental consequences for his future. Still, sitting backstage at his table, away from the fifteen thousand fans who had paid $15 each to attend the draft, Steve felt strangely as if he weren't even at the event at all.

Steve watched on the video monitors in the Green Room as Commissioner David Stern announced Allen Iverson's name as the number-one overall pick by the Philadelphia 76ers. No surprise there. Iverson was clearly the biggest name in this draft. The Vancouver Grizzlies took Shareef Abdur-Rahim at number three, ending any wild speculation that they might use that pick to draft Nash. Again, no big surprise.

But Steve started to feel his stomach tighten after Stephon Marbury went fourth overall to the Milwaukee Bucks five minutes later. That left the Canadian as the highest-rated point guard among remaining players.

Steve had thought there was a chance that the Minnesota Timberwolves, who were looking for a point guard and had been impressed by his pre-draft visit, might call his name at number five. But the T-Wolves took Connecticut shooting guard Ray Allen, whom they would subsequently swap to the Bucks for Marbury. A few picks later, Indiana, which had also been rumored to be highly interested in Steve, took center Erick Dampier of Mississippi State with the number-ten selection. The anxiety level for the remaining players was climbing with every selection.

Steve steeled himself again when it came time for the thirteenth pick, by the Charlotte Hornets, another team that had seemed keen on him. But the Hornets instead opted for the high-schooler Kobe Bryant, whom they would subsequently trade to the Los Angeles Lakers.

The Sacramento Kings used the number-fourteen pick to select Peja Stojakovic, a sharpshooting forward from Serbia and Montenegro who had played in the Greek pro league the previous season. The next four teams to pick, in order, were Phoenix, Charlotte, Portland, and New York, each of whom Steve had visited before the draft. He wasn't worried; Steve was reasonably confident he would go to one of those franchises. John and Jean Nash, meanwhile, sat nervously beside him, simply hoping their son wouldn't be disappointed on a night for which he had worked so long and hard.

Now, suddenly, the cameraman was moving toward the Nash table. And Steve immediately realized why. On the TV monitor, David Stern was already heading toward the microphone to announce the next pick. Steve's heart raced as the camera lens fixed on him.

"With the fifteenth pick in the 1996 NBA draft, the Phoenix Suns select Steve Nash of the University of Santa Clara," the commissioner said.

With the words he had waited years to hear, Steve immediately rose to find his mother. "You're a wonderful mom and you've helped me so much," he said, wrapping Jean in an emotional embrace.

Martin Nash bounced up from the table to hug his big brother, accidentally bumping his mom into the chair behind her. Only the quick action of Nancy Miller, the mother of Steve's high school buddy Jamie, broke her fall. As a result, however, Jean didn't even see her eldest son ascend the stage to officially join the world's best basketball league.

Steve was surprised by the size of the crowd in the arena as he turned the corner from the Green Room onto the draft stage. An NBA staffer had already handed him a white cap with "Suns" lettered across the front in red. He placed it on his head and walked slowly and deliberately up the short set of stairs toward David Stern. As he made his way across the stage, Steve pumped his fists and flashed a brilliant, wide-eyed smile. It was a look filled with pure joy and the satisfaction of a dream realized.

Steve was moving slowly, partly because of the magnitude of this moment but mostly because he was trying to pick out his friends in the arena crowd. He saw them, directly in line with the commissioner's head—Jake Sedlock, Drew Zurek, Kevin Dunne, and Phil Von Buchwaldt from his Santa Clara team. And mixed among those Broncos was a pack of longtime buddies from back home in Victoria, the guys with whom he had grown up and first fallen in love with the game of basketball—Jamie Miller, Al Whitley, Adam Miller, John Clancy, Chris Isherwood, and Brent McLay. Despite the size of the crowd, the hoots and hollers from Nash's personal cheering section could be heard all the way up on stage.

"Wow, you've got a rowdy group of followers," the commissioner said as he welcomed Nash into the NBA.

"Yeah, they came all the way from Canada," Steve grinned.

After brief interview sessions with TNT and ESPN Radio, Steve found his contingent of buddies along the boards of the arena. The entire gang reached over the glass and mobbed him, grabbing his shoulders and arms and rocking Steve back and forth in celebration. They were enjoying this moment as much as he was, and Steve was delighted that they could all be there to share it with him.

With his selection at number fifteen, the highest a Canadian player had ever been drafted in the NBA, Steve had made Canadian basketball history. The next closest was Bill Wennington, who had been the sixteenth pick in 1985. In the previous forty-seven years, only twenty

Canadians had been drafted in total, and since the draft had been capped at two rounds in 1989, only two other Canadians had been selected.

Where he stacked up in the draft history of his country didn't matter much to Steve, however. What was important was that he was in the NBA. The goal he had harbored since Grade 8 had been realized. He had made it. "This is just a dream come true and it's unbelievable," a grinning Steve told reporters covering the draft.

"I hope the kids back home in Canada will be able to look at my success and be able to transfer that into their own path. I hope they will be able to relate to me and to understand what it takes to be successful and that they'll be able to feed off my success and my path and my struggle."

With his selection came instant financial security. Steve's family already lived a comfortable existence in Victoria, but this would take him to another financial echelon altogether. The NBA's rookie salary structure would guarantee Steve a total of US$3.2 million over the next three years. After spending the last four years as a college student, suddenly not having to worry about money for the foreseeable future was an awfully nice fringe benefit to his dream.

Just minutes after the greatest moment of his young life, however, Steve dealt with his first taste of adversity as a professional athlete. Reporters noted that the Suns already had All-Star Kevin Johnson and backup Elliot Perry on their roster at point guard. Did Steve expect to be traded before he had even played a minute in Phoenix?

Next came news that was decidedly more troubling. Steve soon learned through reporters from Phoenix that his selection hadn't gone over well with fans at a draft party being staged by the Suns at America West Arena. Fans at the Phoenix party had actually booed his selection after it was announced by Suns assistant coach Danny Ainge. Many Suns supporters had wanted the team to take Syracuse University forward John Wallace, who had starred for the Orangemen during the NCAA Final Four that spring. Wallace's stock had fallen in the days leading up to the draft and he had surprisingly still been available when it came time for Phoenix to pick. When the Suns instead opted for Nash, a small, Canadian point guard who, compared to Wallace, was relatively unknown, the fans in Phoenix weren't happy.

"The fans here booed you. How does it feel?" reporters from Arizona asked Steve.

Obviously, it didn't feel great. Like anybody in his position, Steve would have preferred to be welcomed warmly by his future home crowd. But he understood how things worked. John Wallace was a much bigger name. It was natural fans who had never seen Steve play would be disappointed.

"I'm glad they booed," Steve replied. "It showed that they're passionate about their team. I probably would have booed myself, too."

Suns owner Jerry Colangelo wasn't worried about the fans' reaction. They had booed forward Dan Majerle and guard Michael Finley in similar circumstances when they were drafted, and both those players had proven to be stars and fan favorites in Phoenix. "A lot of people like to talk about what a player can't do," Colangelo told reporters on draft night. "Let's talk about what Nash can do: he's a good distributor of the ball, he can shoot from the perimeter, and he's a leader."

"I think he's a player who will be better in the NBA than he was in college because he's the type of player who makes other guys around him better," Ainge added.

As his first training camp approached that fall in Flagstaff, Arizona, Steve knew he would again be facing some stiff challenges. But he remained confident that he would eventually prove any doubters wrong. When he was asked during an introductory Phoenix press conference what kind of player he would be in the NBA, Steve joked: "Probably a little bit like Michael Jordan at first."

"I might be horrible the first three months," he told a friend, on a more serious note, shortly after draft day. "But I'm going to get better every single day. I'm going to raise my game to that level. I know that if there is something I need to work on, like there always has been before, I'll work on it and I'll get it done."

8

CALL ME "ROOK"

"You've got to prove yourself all over again."

—Steve Nash, NBA rookie, 1996–97

The first thing Steve Nash did when he joined the Phoenix Suns for his inaugural professional training camp at Flagstaff, Arizona, was say goodbye to his name. As far as veteran Phoenix head coach Cotton Fitzsimmons was concerned, he was now simply "Rook."

While the Suns organization warmly welcomed their new first-round draft pick in October 1996, it was abundantly clear to Steve that nothing would be handed to him as he began his NBA career. He was a third-stringer at point guard on the Phoenix depth chart, and, for the first time in his basketball career, it seemed certain he would not be playing a significant role for his team during the coming season.

Many fans still didn't understand why the Suns would choose him when they already had a franchise point guard in Kevin Johnson. Steve had known since the June draft that Johnson was going to play at least one more season with the Suns before retiring. And thanks to a pre-season blockbuster trade that had sent superstar Charles Barkley to the Houston Rockets, the Canadian rookie was now also playing behind newly acquired veteran Sam Cassell. Steve was well aware that playing time was not going to come easily, particularly under the old-school Fitzsimmons.

Still, there were plenty of reasons to be optimistic. First of all, the mere fact that he was in the NBA was enough to put a permanent smile on Steve's face. He had already come farther than just about anybody had predicted, and, the way he looked at it, he was actually in a terrific situation, being able to learn behind two experienced and talented point guards. Steve felt as though he could afford to be patient in Phoenix; there was no rush for him to become a starter.

It did require a mental adjustment, however. After starring throughout junior high and high school and for the past three NCAA seasons, he would now have to concentrate on turning in strong performances on the practice floor. In many games he would have to accept the fact that he wouldn't see the court at all. But as Steve approached his first season, he was determined to enjoy the experience, no matter what happened. His job seemed simple enough—he would pay his dues, work hard in practice, make the most of his limited playing time, and generally learn how to be a pro basketball player.

In the weeks leading up to training camp, Steve had settled nicely into Phoenix, renting a comfortable condo in the Gainey Ranch resort within the upscale suburb of Scottsdale. It was a large, three-bedroom place, with his master suite window overlooking an inviting turquoise pool and lush golf course. Two of Steve's old high school teammates from Victoria, Chris Isherwood and Jamie Miller, were rooming with him for the year, keeping him company. Isherwood was working with his father in the real estate business in Phoenix and Miller had just finished playing a single season of NCAA basketball at Colorado, where he had made the team as a walk-on. Steve's mother, Jean, now acting as his business agent, had even lined up a cook to prepare the meals Steve would be too busy to make for himself.

Despite the fact that he had signed a contract paying him US$763,000 for his first season, Steve still hadn't bought his own car as the season approached. He could take care of that detail soon enough, he figured. What he wanted to concentrate on was making sure he was ready to compete in training camp and to prepare himself for the grind of an eighty-two-game regular schedule. Although he would be playing limited time as a rookie, Steve knew there would be no "easy ones" in the NBA. In college, every couple of games he had faced a point guard who couldn't go to his left, couldn't shoot, or was slow. There would be no nights off like that in the pros. Even as a Suns reserve, he would have to be prepared every night for the challenge of meeting John Stockton, Nick Van Exel, Gary Payton, and Jason Kidd.

Steve would have to learn quickly about eating well on the road and getting enough sleep. In the coming NBA season, including exhibitions and possibly playoffs, the Suns might play more than a hundred games. That was more than triple what he had played in the average season with Santa Clara over the past four years, and almost as many games as he had compiled during his entire four-year career at the California college. And the travel, with the Suns criss-crossing North America, would be far more taxing than it had been as a Bronco.

Life as an NBA player was, essentially, life out of a suitcase. The Suns traveled in style, though. Phoenix had a private jet, well stocked with food and fitted out with generous seats that afforded enough leg room for seven-footers. Every player's place on the plane included a private video screen with a large selection of movies. If you had to be on the go all the time, this was the way to do it, Steve thought.

Despite the travel, Steve soon found himself slipping comfortably into the lifestyle of an NBA player, particularly when the Suns were at home. Now there were no classes to attend, and, being single with no children, Steve had plenty of free time outside the few hours of practice and training required each day. Phoenix was chock-full of great golf courses and the weather was superb.

The biggest challenge was simply learning to compete at the NBA level, where everybody was bigger and stronger and the play was much faster. As a point guard, he now had to make decisions with the basketball much more quickly than he had in college. For the first couple of weeks of training camp and exhibitions he struggled, but soon after that the twenty-two-year-old found himself adjusting to the new pace and strength of the opposition.

As training camp and the pre-season passed, however, Steve still had much to learn—about the Suns' complicated triangle offense and especially about playing defense in the NBA. With starter Kevin Johnson sidelined for the first few weeks after undergoing hernia surgery, Steve found himself going up in practice against Sam Cassell, a veteran who had won two NBA championships with the Houston Rockets. He and Cassell quickly became friends, and it was a boost to Steve's confidence when Cassell took the time to talk with Steve after practices about how he could improve his game. The way Steve saw it, Cassell wouldn't waste his time if he didn't believe a rookie had some serious potential.

Steve's adjustment was also hastened by the fact that he got much more playing time in the exhibition season than he had expected, due to Johnson's surgery. Over eight pre-season games, he averaged an encouraging twenty-two minutes on the court. There were lessons to learn about the pro game, however. In his NBA exhibition debut against the visiting Vancouver Grizzlies, Steve was assessed four fouls in just seven first-half minutes, giving the veterans on the Phoenix bench a chuckle at the expense of their well-liked, wide-eyed rookie.

Steve opened some eyes in the Suns' final pre-season game at Mexico City when he went up against future Utah Jazz Hall-of-Famer John Stockton, a pro to whom he had often been compared by scouts and college coaches. In forty-five minutes of action, Steve nearly recorded a triple-double with 20 points, 11 assists, and 7 rebounds.

Steve knew the minutes on the court would dry up when the real games began. Still, he was excited as his NBA regular-season debut approached on November 1, 1996. Not only was it his first official pro game, it was also the Los Angeles debut of massive center Shaquille O'Neal, who had joined the Lakers over the summer from the Orlando Magic in the biggest NBA off-season move in several years. "The fact that my first game will be in the Forum, which is such a great atmosphere, and with all those celebrities there, makes it that much more exciting. Now with Shaq there, too, it's going to just be magnified. It's going to be a lot of fun," Steve told a friend on the day his pro career officially began.

Playing behind Cassell and Rex Chapman, Steve saw five minutes of floor time in his debut at Los Angeles. He was scoreless with one missed three-point attempt. The next night, in his first NBA home game against the Houston Rockets, he scored 8 points, recorded his first three-pointer and his first assist, and began to win over some of the skeptical Suns fans in America West Arena.

As expected, playing time was sparse during that rookie season, with one notable exception. And as far as Steve was concerned, it couldn't have come at a better time, as the Suns were in Vancouver for a November 14 game against the Grizzlies.

British Columbia basketball fans had anticipated this game for months, as it marked the first time Nash would play professionally in his home province. Steve was inundated with ticket requests from more than fifty friends and family, and Grizzlies owner Arthur Griffiths graciously gave up his courtside seats so that John and Jean Nash could watch their son's "home debut" in style.

The Suns also made the event special by holding a press conference specifically to highlight Nash at the luxurious Pan Pacific Hotel in downtown Vancouver the day before the game.

"I'm really glad to be back home and it's nice to see a lot of familiar faces," Nash told the media. "I can honestly say that I've never been to the Pan Pacific, so this is kind of nice, too … I don't think they would have let me in here four years ago."

Steve's Phoenix teammates seemed to get a huge kick out of their rookie's celebrity status. Center Danny Manning playfully sang "O Canada" as his young teammate conducted countless interviews during the Suns' morning shoot-around the next day. And as hordes of home-province reporters followed Steve around General Motors Place, Manning cracked, "Can I still join in on the Steve Nash Historical Tour?"

In an unlikely scenario, Suns coach Cotton Fitzsimmons appeared at Steve's press conference to talk specifically about a rookie who figured to barely see the floor that season. Fitzsimmons' Suns were winless in seven games to that point in the schedule, and the coach had more important things to concern himself with than whether the "Rook's" return home went smoothly.

"I'd like to put him in the game here," Fitzsimmons told the media gathered for Steve's press conference. "But if somebody else is doing a better job, I'm going to sit him down right next to me and tell his parents I'm sorry."

No apologies were necessary, as it turned out. With Johnson still sidelined and Sam Cassell suddenly out with a timely case of the flu, Fitzsimmons had little choice but to give Steve the first start of his NBA career in Vancouver. Steve felt goosebumps on his arms and a rush of pride as he received a huge ovation while being introduced to the Vancouver crowd. And although nervous before tip-off, the rookie responded in dramatic fashion, scoring 17 points and adding 12 assists and 7 rebounds in forty-six minutes. The only downside to his home debut was the fact that the Suns lost 92–89 to the Grizzlies, who had also been winless going into the game.

While in Vancouver, Fitzsimmons announced he was stepping down as Suns coach, relinquishing the job to assistant Danny Ainge. This move was seen by most as positive news for Steve. During a long career with the Boston Celtics, Sacramento Kings, Portland Trail Blazers, and Phoenix Suns, Ainge had been a player with a style similar to Nash's, and he had also been one of the driving forces behind the Suns' selection of Steve in the 1996 draft.

Regardless, the Vancouver game was easily the highlight of Steve's 1996–97 season. He also played in the NBA All-Rookie game as part of All-Star Weekend at Cleveland in February, but, for the most part, he rode the bench, averaging just 3.3 points and 2.1 assists in third-stringer minutes for the Suns.

While the apprenticeship was something he'd expected, Steve was not prepared for the shock he received on Boxing Day of that rookie season. Sitting in his Phoenix living room, watching an NBA game on television, he discovered, along with thousands of other basketball fans, that the Suns had swung a major trade, acquiring star point guard Jason Kidd in a six-player swap with the Dallas Mavericks.

Although Sam Cassell had been shipped out of Phoenix in the deal, the acquisition of Kidd and the continued presence of Johnson suddenly left Steve sitting behind not one but two All-Stars at his position. He had been playing well to that point in the season and everybody in the organization seemed positive about his progress, so Steve was surprised that the Suns would trade for yet another point guard. He was also shocked to see three teammates—Sam Cassell, Michael Finley, and A. C. Green—gone in the blink of an eye. It was his first real taste of the business side of basketball. *It's sad,* Steve thought at the time. *You just get close to three guys and all of a sudden they're gone.*

While he realized that landing Kidd, who two years earlier had shared the NBA Rookie of the Year honor with Grant Hill, was a smart move for the Suns, Steve knew this would mean even less time for him during his rookie season. He also naturally wondered what it meant for his own long-term prospects in Phoenix. With this move, the Suns had instantly altered his status as the franchise's point guard of the future.

There was nothing Steve could do about it, however, except to make the best of the situation. He would now be playing behind two of the finest point guards in the NBA. There was a lot he could learn from them. "I knew I wasn't as good as those guys," he would reflect years later, "and I thought it was a great opportunity to closely monitor my progress toward their ability and level."

Steve also enjoyed where he was playing. The city and the weather were great, and so were the fans. The Suns had gone 0–13 to start his rookie season, but the team had nevertheless drawn a sellout of 19,023 fans for every game. The fans who had once booed the team's decision to draft him were now clamoring for his autograph. Despite his status as a third-string rookie, the lineup to get Steve's signature during a December appearance at a suburban store had snaked out the doorway and run nearly the length of the mall. He had even had the "Steve Nash Rookie Burger" named in his honor at Majerle's, a popular downtown eatery owned by former Sun Dan Majerle. Phoenix was probably the best basketball city in the world as far as Steve was concerned.

By the spring of 1997, trade rumors involving Steve had already begun to circulate. Those only escalated after Kevin Johnson announced he would return for yet another season in 1997–98, postponing his expected retirement by a year.

Among the teams interested in Steve were the Vancouver Grizzlies. But Vancouver passed up a second opportunity to land the homegrown guard when they rejected a Phoenix trade offer packaging Steve and another veteran for their number-four pick in the June 1997 draft. That selection turned out to be journeyman guard Antonio Daniels, whom Vancouver would trade after just one season.

"I suggested to [Grizzlies general manager] Stu Jackson at the time that he bring home one of B.C.'s greats," Suns president Bryan Colangelo would tell *The Vancouver Sun* years later. "I thought it would be a great story and I thought it made a lot of sense for their franchise—a natural fit. I certainly tried to sell it for Stu that Steve would have been a lightning rod for a successful operation. He clearly was a guy who was popular and a cult hero from that area of the world and we thought there were a lot of things that made sense."

Logical or not, the Grizzlies balked at giving up their fourth overall pick in exchange for Steve, in what will go down as one of the biggest mistakes ever made by a major professional sports franchise.

With Steve remaining in Phoenix for his second NBA season, the general consensus was that, despite all his potential, the young Canadian might play even less as a sophomore pro than he had as a rookie.

Steve heard those theories, but he had different ideas. He felt he had improved tremendously since coming into the league and he was motivated to try to break into head coach Danny Ainge's lineup, no matter who was playing ahead of him. He split the summer of 1997 between the weight room and the gym, as well as helping Canada to qualify for the following year's World Championship Tournament. He worked on getting better at shooting off screens, so he would be more prepared to play shooting guard, figuring that was a way he could get additional minutes in the Phoenix rotation.

Steve got a shot of confidence after a training camp workout in the fall of 1997, when Kevin Johnson approached him in the Suns' locker room. The three-time NBA All-Star was shaking his head.

"What's up?" Steve asked the veteran.

"You just don't know how good you are," Johnson replied with a smile.

"You think so?" Steve said.

"I know so." Johnson nodded. "In the last ten years or so, I've probably seen thirty great guards in this league. You're up there with all of them. One day you'll know that."

Coach Danny Ainge also stoked Steve's confidence as the season approached. "He's going to get a chance to play," Ainge told *The Arizona Republic*. "That little sucker can play. Everybody is starting to believe me now."

"I might still be on the bench," Steve said as his second NBA season dawned. "But I know it's not because I'm not ready to play."

Steve proved he was indeed ready during that 1997–98 season, playing so well that Ainge often went to a three-guard lineup just to get him some minutes. As an NBA sophomore, Nash averaged 9.1 points and 3.4 assists and was even used at times by Ainge as a defensive stopper, something nobody would have predicted when he'd entered the league. Although he had always felt wanted since joining the Suns organization, in this second year he felt needed, too.

"That might have been as big an accomplishment as I'd had in my career. Under those circumstances, I played over twenty minutes a game that season, with two Hall of Fame point guards ahead of me," Steve says now. "It was a turning point for me in some ways, where I could really see my work pay off and see the improvement and believe that I could play with these guys."

Steve's improvement left both him and the Suns in a difficult position as his second season concluded. With his rookie contract set to expire the following year, Phoenix management wanted to sign him to an extension that would keep him with the club for several more seasons. But with Jason Kidd firmly entrenched as the starting Phoenix point guard, it was clear the Suns weren't going to offer Steve the kind of contract given to front-line guards in the NBA.

Steve, meanwhile, believed he was good enough to start at point guard and run his own team. Nine other NBA teams also thought so, as they made trade overtures to the Suns. Included in that group were the Vancouver Grizzlies and the Dallas Mavericks.

When Steve declined to sign a lesser contract with the Suns, Phoenix decided it had better get something in exchange for him while it could. So on the day the 1998 NBA draft was being held in Vancouver, the Suns swung a trade, sending Steve to Dallas in exchange for forwards Pat Garrity, Bubba Wells, Martin Muursepp, and a future first-round draft pick that would ultimately turn out to be forward Shawn Marion.

Steve was in England visiting relatives and had already gone to bed when his mother called long-distance to inform him about the trade. He wasn't completely surprised. He and agent Bill Duffy had known that there was a good chance of something happening during the off-season. They just hadn't been sure where he would be going or when.

"At some point, this was probably inevitable," Steve said on the day of the draft. "Something like this was going to happen. I've sort of put myself in the position where I can command a starting point guard salary and the starting point guard role."

The move, though mutually agreed upon, was a difficult one for Steve. "I felt really at home in Phoenix," he says now. "I naively felt a lot of loyalty. And you know it's not a business that's built on loyalty. So, I was a little disappointed because I'd really made friends and fit in and felt good there and enjoyed everyone in the organization. But at the end of the day it's about your career. If you don't look out for your career, no one else really is going to."

Though sad to leave Phoenix, the franchise that had brought him into the NBA, Steve was excited about the new opportunity in Texas. He would be joining athletic swingman Michael Finley, with whom he had been a teammate and become good friends during his rookie season. The Mavericks had also picked up an interesting draft choice that same day, getting German teenager Dirk Nowitzki, who some were whispering had the potential to be the next Larry Bird. The Mavericks had missed the playoffs for eight straight seasons, but Steve had the feeling he could help turn things around in Dallas.

The Mavericks, led by the father-and-son team of Don and Donnie Nelson, were familiar with Steve's game. Both Nelsons had coached in Golden State when Nash had starred at nearby Santa Clara. And Donnie Nelson had served as an assistant coach during Steve's first season in Phoenix. They were confident he was capable of much more than the nearly seventeen minutes, 6.4 points, and 2.8 assists a game he had averaged over his first two NBA seasons as a Sun.

Dallas was so confident, in fact, that it signed Steve Nash to a six-year, US$33-million contract extension before he had played a single minute for the franchise. "That's a terrific feeling for me," Steve told reporters in Dallas. "Unless they trade me for Shaq, I'm going to be here a long time." Don Nelson then promptly named him a starter and co-captain of the Mavericks along with Michael Finley.

As Steve moved on to Dallas in the summer of 1998, it seemed his apprenticeship as an NBA point guard was over. The time had come to make his mark.

9

DOG DAYS IN DALLAS

"You've just got to do the things you've always done and don't let your life hinge on shots going in or out."

—Steve Nash, struggling Dallas Maverick, 1999

He heard them immediately as he checked into the game from the scorer's table. Just a small smattering at first, but within seconds the sound had grown into an unmistakable sonic wave, easily distinguishable even in the din of Dallas's Reunion Arena. Steve Nash was being booed.

It was March 24, 1999, late in the third quarter of a game against the visiting Houston Rockets. So far, Steve had missed all eight shots he had attempted. Once again, the Mavericks were struggling, as they had been for much of this dismal NBA season. The disenchanted in Dallas had seen enough.

Steve felt his ears burning as he slowly realized that the boos were aimed directly at him. It was the first time in his career that he had ever been singled out during a game for such harsh treatment by his own fans. He had been heckled on the road in college countless times, and opposing fans had even targeted him on a few occasions in high school. But coming from the home crowd, this hurt. Nobody on the team was playing well, and Steve realized that the fans were bitterly disappointed to be suffering through yet another losing season, but he hadn't expected to be singled out as the focal point of their frustration.

This night was simply the culmination of what had been a horrible first season for Steve and the Mavericks. After the excitement of the draft-day deal the previous June and the promise of becoming an NBA starter, there had been a series of increasingly disappointing developments. First came the NBA labor lockout, which had delayed the start of his initial season in Dallas and condensed it to just fifty games. Next there had been a rash of injuries—a painful case of plantar fasciitis, sometimes called a "heel spur," that had lingered throughout the summer and into the fall, a broken nose, an upper respiratory ailment, and a slipped vertebra in his back, which years later would be identified as a congenital condition—all of which had combined to severely limit his effectiveness.

"It's funny, the little things that you forget," Steve would recall years later. "I had a cut on my middle finger on my shooting hand. So for a lot of that season, I was trying not to touch the ball with my finger when I shot. And you know, you don't tell many people that and make excuses. But looking back, that's probably not the best, most successful way to shoot a basketball."

The result of all those physical problems was that Steve was suffering through a terrible shooting slump that had begun with a 3-for-13 night in a season-opening loss in Seattle and had rarely subsided. Shots that felt good as they left his hand were mysteriously rimming out or falling off the iron and he didn't know why. Absolutely nothing was going right.

It certainly wasn't what Steve had hoped for when he'd been traded to the Mavericks the previous June. And it wasn't what Dallas fans had expected after coach and general manager Don Nelson had dealt four players for the promising backup with the Phoenix Suns. Nelson had confidently told the Dallas media that Steve Nash was the kind of point guard he could build a team around, and the veteran basketball man had even predicted that, with Steve and Michael Finley leading the way, the woeful Mavericks would make the playoffs for the first time in nine seasons. Nelson had signed Steve to a US$33-million contract, a deal many felt was too generous for a player still unproven as a starter in the NBA. "I'm certain he's a very good player," Nelson had told reporters before the belated regular season began in February. "He's got the whole package."

Fans in Dallas hadn't seen that package yet, however. Steve realized it more than anybody and was frustrated that he hadn't been able to prove his worth to the Mavericks and their supporters. As this first season with Dallas headed toward a merciful close, Steve was making just 35 percent of his shots, by far the worst shooting season since he had first picked up a basketball. And his nagging injuries certainly weren't helping, as they prevented him from feeling properly balanced on his shot and slowed him just enough to make it much more difficult to beat his defenders off the dribble. The fact that he was trying to live up to the huge contract he had signed with the Mavericks was also causing him to press more than usual and getting in the way of the confident creativity necessary for him to play at his best. The bottom line was that he wasn't the player he had been in his second NBA season with the Suns.

Just a few days before the game against Houston, teammate Cedric Ceballos, who had also played with Steve on the Suns, pulled him aside during a practice. "You don't look like the guy I played with in Phoenix," he told Nash. "You're putting too much pressure on yourself instead of just playing with reckless abandon."

Steve tried his best to ignore the boo-birds as he entered this March game against the Rockets. But that became impossible to do as every single time he touched the ball, the boos rained down from the stands. It was embarrassing and obvious to everybody in the building. Just two games earlier, he had scored 22 points and been cheered by the home crowd in a victory over the Sacramento Kings. Now he was being treated as if he were the Mavericks' most hated opponent. It was difficult not to let it get to him.

Steve looked up into the Reunion Arena stands where Martin was sitting. He wondered how his younger brother, visiting from Vancouver and watching Steve play as a professional for the first time in person, would react to the treatment Steve was now getting from the fans. When he found the familiar face in the crowd, he immediately felt more relaxed. Martin was laughing.

Instantly, his brother's reaction put things in perspective for Steve. *It's not the end of the world,* he was able to tell himself as the game continued. *How many people get to go through this? How many people get booed by a whole arena on their home court? This is a great opportunity for me to overcome something.*

Later, a gesture by Houston's superstar forward Charles Barkley also helped eased the sting. As the players took the floor to start the fourth quarter, Barkley reached out and gave Steve a supportive hug.

Nevertheless, the Dallas fans continued their booing of Nash as the game, an 88–78 loss to the Rockets, wound down. The only time Steve wasn't booed was when he hit a three-pointer with just over six minutes left in the fourth quarter. It had been a miserable night in more ways than one. That three-pointer was the only shot he had successfully made in ten attempts.

Afterward, reporters wanted to know how Steve had felt about being treated so harshly by the Mavericks fans. The truth was, he still felt hurt. He had been working hard to turn things around, both for himself and for the struggling Dallas franchise. This experience certainly hadn't helped. But Steve managed to put on a brave face for the media.

"The fans pay money to come watch us play and they have every right to cheer us, to boo us, or to have any reaction that they please," he told reporters. "I didn't play

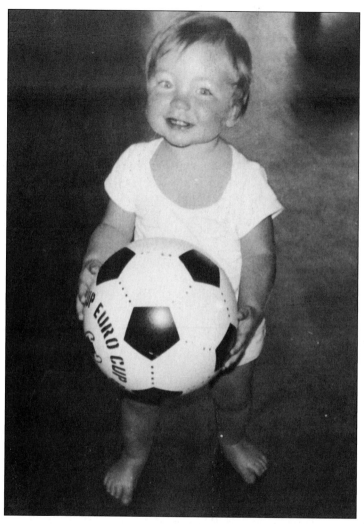

Even as a toddler, Steve Nash was fixated on sports. His mother,
Jean, remembers he would play only with sports equipment.
Soccer was young Steve's early love, and the first word out of his
mouth was "Gooaallllll!" Steve's father, John, believes Steve's
soccer training played an important role in developing
the tremendous balance and footwork that are now
essential parts of his basketball skill set.
(Photo: Nash family)

Steve Nash was a standout in minor soccer as a young boy growing up in Victoria. He came by his talent for the game honestly. His father, John, was a semiprofessional player in South Africa, his brother, Martin, has played 30 times internationally for Canada, and his sister, Joann, was captain of the University of Victoria women's team for three years.
(Photo: Nash family)

The 1991–92 St. Michaels University School Blue Devils compiled
one of the most impressive seasons in B.C. high school basketball
history, going 50–4 and winning the provincial AAA title.
Here, the team is pictured celebrating the championship win
on the floor of the Agrodome. Included in the photo are
Steve Nash (mid-picture, holding the corner of the banner
with one finger in the air) and head coach Ian Hyde-Lay
(mid-picture, standing and holding a framed photo).
(Photo: Preston Yip)

Steve Nash brings up the ball against a Brigham Young University
defender during the championship game of the Santa Clara Broncos'
annual Cable Car Classic tournament on December 29, 1994,
in the San Jose Arena. Steve scored 22 points in this game, which
came early in his junior season with Santa Clara, but the Broncos
fell 76–55. Steve enjoyed an outstanding junior season, winning his
first of two consecutive West Coast Conference Most Valuable Player
awards and leading the Broncos into the NCAA Tournament.
(Photo: Santa Clara University)

Just seconds after being selected fifteenth overall
in the 1996 NBA draft at East Rutherford, New Jersey,
Steve Nash's face reflects the excitement of realizing
a childhood dream. With his selection by the Phoenix Suns,
Steve became the highest-drafted Canadian in NBA history.
(Photo: CP/AP/Kathy Willens)

In his first two NBA seasons with the Phoenix Suns, Steve Nash
quickly became a fan favorite, despite seeing limited time
on the court playing behind a pair of All-Star point guards.
Here he gets airborne to keep the ball from flying out
of bounds during a game at Atlanta in the 1997–98 season.
(Photo: CP/AP/Erik S. Lesser)

Wearing the Canadian uniform in international play has always
been a source of tremendous pride for Steve Nash, shown here
with his parents, John and Jean, prior to a game on the road
to the 2000 Olympics in Sydney, Australia. Steve turned in
a phenomenal performance in those Olympics as Canada's
floor general, leading the national team to a surprising
5–2 record and narrowly missing a shot at the podium.
(Photo: Nash family)

Fighting for a loose ball with a much larger Shaquille O'Neal is
Steve Nash, during the 2001–2002 season with the Dallas Mavericks.
Although by this point he had emerged as a valuable star for the
Mavericks, few could have predicted that Steve would edge O'Neal
for the NBA's Most Valuable Player award just three years later.
(Photo: CP/AP/Donna McWilliam)

Steve Nash, shown here during the 2003 Western Conference finals with the Dallas Mavericks, prepares to drive on San Antonio Spurs guard Tony Parker. During ten professional seasons Steve has been to the conference finals three times, but he is still looking for his first trip to the NBA's championship series.
(Photo: CP/AP/David J. Phillip)

The Dallas Mavericks' "Big Three" included Michael Finley (4),
Dirk Nowitzki (41), and Steve Nash (13). The talented trio powered
the team's rise from one of the worst franchises in the NBA to one
of the best. The "Big Three" was split up in 2004 when Nash left
Dallas to sign a free-agent deal with the Phoenix Suns. Finley joined
the San Antonio Spurs in 2005. Only Nowitzki remains a Maverick.
(Photo: Nash family)

Making a move on Chicago's Ben Gordon during a game in
November 2004 is Steve Nash. Despite the belief of some scouts
that he didn't possess the quickness or athleticism to beat NBA
defenders, Steve has become a dominant offensive force in the
league. During his second straight MVP season in 2005–2006,
he averaged more than 18 points and 10 assists per game.
(Photo: CP/AP/Brian Kersey)

Steve Nash shares a friendly high-five with a young fan during his inaugural summer charity game in Toronto's Air Canada Centre in July 2005. Nash later brought the game to Vancouver's General Motors Place in July 2006. Proceeds from the two games and related activities went to the Steve Nash Foundation, which has helped underserved youth since 2001.
(Photo: CP/Adrian Wyld)

Steve Nash hoists the Maurice Podoloff Trophy, presented annually to the NBA's Most Valuable Player, prior to a May 8, 2006, playoff game in Phoenix against the Los Angeles Clippers. Steve never dreamed of winning the prestigious award once, let alone twice in back-to-back seasons. But he would happily trade both those honors for an NBA championship ring with the Suns.
(Photo: CP/AP/Matt York)

While he is considered among the best outside shooters in the NBA,
Steve Nash gets many of his points in the paint on drives such as the
one he makes here on Vladimir Radmanovic of the Los Angeles
Clippers during the second round of the 2006 NBA playoffs. Nash's
ability to finish inside against much bigger defenders is a key
component in his offensive arsenal.
(Photo: CP/AP/Matt York)

Steve Nash prepares to lay in the basketball despite the efforts of good friend and Dallas Mavericks superstar Dirk Nowitzki during Game 6 of the 2006 NBA Western Conference finals. It was the second straight post-season matchup between the two buddies, who were longtime teammates in Dallas. So far, the playoff encounters between Nash's Suns and Nowitzki's Mavericks have been evenly split, with each team winning one series.
(Photo: CP/AP/Matt York)

Good friends Steve Nash and Dirk Nowitzki embrace on the court
following the Dallas Mavericks' series-clinching 102–93 victory
over the Phoenix Suns in Game 6 of the 2006 NBA Western
Conference finals. So much has changed for the pair since
their early struggles together in Dallas, and they are now two
of the most recognizable names and faces in pro basketball.
(Photo: CP/AP/Matt York)

well. I didn't shoot the ball well and they weren't happy about it, and they showed their displeasure and that's fine."

Other players, even those on the Rockets, disagreed, however. Teammate Michael Finley ripped the Dallas fans, saying he didn't appreciate their behavior. "True fans of any sport, you don't boo the home team," he said. "When things are going downhill like they were—not only for Steve, but for the team—that's the time when fans should be behind a team or an individual and cheer for them more. But to hear them boo our own player, I was very disappointed."

"I'm very disappointed in the Dallas fans," added Charles Barkley. "He's a good kid. I like him a lot. Why don't they send him down to Houston? We'll take him."

Don Nelson, the sometimes gruff coach and general manager who had brought Steve to Dallas and staked much of his reputation on the point guard panning out for the Mavericks, told reporters after the game that Nash had to grow up and get tougher.

"We know he's a much better player than he's playing," Nelson said. "He's got to toughen up, that's all. He's got to prove to people that he's a player. If it takes hitting the bottom of the barrel, which maybe he did tonight, then let's see."

As far as Steve was concerned, this disappointing turn of events represented a new challenge. He would get healthy, work on his shot, and prove to these people that they were wrong to boo him. He would show everybody in Dallas that he was a starting point guard in the NBA and a good one. Despite the unpleasant experience in this game, Steve was still confident he could do that. *You've just got to do the things you've always done and don't let your life hinge on shots going in or out,* he told himself.

"I still feel confident. I still feel I'm going to become a really good player," Steve told reporters. "One day, good things are going to happen for me and this team. I've always been kind of a fan favorite, not a goat, so it's a new challenge for me. The fans can continue to voice their displeasure, but … I can't apologize, because I'm working my butt off. I'm trying my hardest."

Plenty of support from back home in Victoria through phone calls and e-mails helped. His former high school coach Ian Hyde-Lay e-mailed Steve to remind him that "good players don't turn bad overnight." Teammates also helped ease the tension with humor. During a practice the same week, fellow Mavericks Hubert Davis and Erick Strickland took turns playfully booing Steve as they were all squaring off in a free-throw-shooting contest. Steve also took comfort in the fact that Dallas Cowboys Hall of Fame quarterback Troy Aikman had once been booed at Reunion Arena when he was introduced to the crowd during a losing National Football League season.

"There's going to be a point," Steve told a friend after the booing incident, "when this will all be forgotten and this will all be just a bump in the road. I'm willing to accept responsibility—I haven't played well. I'm subject to criticism. That's fine and I understand it. All I can do is work hard on every aspect of my game."

As the 1999 NBA campaign wore down, Steve described it as "the worst season of my life." But over time he would look back on that season as another valuable learning experience in his NBA career. He learned he had to listen to his body more closely and to sit out when he was too hurt to play. He also learned just how fickle fans can be in professional sports.

"It was difficult, but I look at everything as a positive," he says now. "It didn't go well but there was no reason to give up, and I thought I'd learned a lot and faced enough adversity that it could be a positive for me. It taught me about professional sports and fans and people and myself, so it was a great opportunity in some ways."

Also helping to get through that difficult season was Steve's blossoming friendship with Dirk Nowitzki, the twenty-year-old from Germany who had joined the Mavericks that year as well. The two rented apartments in the same complex and soon began traveling together to practice and regularly hanging out.

Steve immediately took a liking to the skinny German seven-footer and wanted to do whatever he could to help him adjust to both life in North America and the rigors of the NBA. They also had a common bond—pressure to live up to great expectations. While Dallas fans were disappointed in Nash's performance during that first year, they were also skeptical about whether Nowitzki would ever be good enough to justify the ninth overall pick they had used in June 1998, taking the German in a deal with Milwaukee instead of Kansas star Paul Pierce. Steve and Dirk faced the daily scrutiny together and learned not to take their situations so seriously.

"I think I helped him," Steve says now. "I mean, he came all the way over [from Europe] at a very young age. I just thought it was easy for me to help a guy and be there for him as a teammate, and it helped me to have somebody there to be a friend with."

Steve sensed immediately that he and Nowitzki could become an effective combination on the basketball court. He loved to pass the ball and Dirk was obviously an outstanding shooter for a seven-footer, even though he didn't immediately show it during NBA games. But he was also very young and it would take the German a while to build up his body and his confidence sufficiently to make an impact.

Steve's first season with Dallas ended unremarkably with the Victoria native sitting out the final ten games because of an injured back. Despite starting forty of the team's fifty games, he had averaged just 7.9 points, down more than a point per game from the previous season in Phoenix. His average of 5.5 assists was respectable, but certainly not the kind of number Dallas fans had been expecting. Meanwhile, Dirk Nowitzki had averaged 8.2 points and 3.4 rebounds as a rookie. As the 1999 season concluded, with the Mavericks winning just nineteen of fifty games, there was still precious little foreshadowing of the dynamic duo they would become for Dallas.

10

"CAPTAIN CANADA"

"I'm really proud to be a part of this team. I wish every-one had the chance to be part of a group like this at some point in their lives."

—Steve Nash, Canadian Olympian, 2000

Steve Nash couldn't hold back the tears as he stood, completely spent and utterly dejected, on the hardwood floor of the Sydney SuperDome following the final buzzer. For one of the few times in his basketball career, he couldn't bring himself to face the media in a post-game press conference.

He had just given everything he had for his country in the quarterfinal round of the 2000 Summer Olympics. But it hadn't been quite enough. His underdog Canadian team had fallen, by a few points, to France, its dreams of capturing an Olympic medal dashed.

But while Steve hadn't won a medal during those Sydney Olympics, he had captured the hearts of Canadian basketball fans with his fearless, leave-it-all-on-the-floor style and his obvious joy in playing for his country. What Steve and his fellow Canadian players had accomplished was impressive, medal or not. They had put Canadian basketball back on the map. And they had prompted thousands of Canadians back home to stay up until the wee hours of the morning to watch something other than ice hockey.

That Canada was even playing in this 2000 Olympic tournament Down Under was in itself a minor miracle. The summer before, Steve had led Team Canada through a qualifying tournament, dubbed "Mission Impossible" by many. Only two berths in the Sydney Olympics were available to North, South, and Central American teams in this qualifying tournament, and one had been virtually conceded to the U.S. lineup, laden with NBA stars. That left Canada with the unenviable task of having to beat out eight other Central and South American squads during a ten-day grind in the summer heat of Puerto Rico.

A keen follower of international basketball, Steve knew what an onerous task the Canadians—with only two NBA players on their roster—faced. Nevertheless, he gave up the entire summer of 1999, shook off the debilitating injuries that had ruined his first season with Dallas, and convinced Mavericks boss Don Nelson to clear him to play for his country.

Steve then proceeded to lead the underdog Canadian squad through the difficult qualifying maze, which concluded with the mighty challenge of having to beat a tough Puerto Rican team on its home court in order to clinch an Olympic berth. In that semifinal game, Steve turned in a performance that national team coach Jay Triano later described as the greatest clutch effort in Canadian basketball history.

In front of more than 15,000 hostile Puerto Rican fans in steamy Roberto Clemente Coliseum, Steve scored 26 points on 10-of-15 shooting and hit five of his seven three-point attempts to power Canada to an 83–71 victory. Despite being slender and not much taller than six-foot-two, he managed to lead all players with 8 rebounds and also chipped in 4 assists in the physical contest. The performance landed a gritty Canadian team its first Olympic men's basketball tournament berth since 1988.

"This is an incredible feeling," Steve told a reporter back in Victoria after the win. "I just hope the kids back home were proud watching it, because we were all proud to be playing for Canada."

Canada did, as expected, fall to the United States, 92–66, in the qualifying tournament championship game. But they had accomplished their goal, and Steve had clearly been the difference. His performance was rewarded with tournament Most Valuable Player honors, ahead of the entire constellation of American NBA stars.

Though the basketball world was impressed with that effort, few gave Steve Nash and Canada much of a chance of getting anywhere close to the podium at the Olympics one year later. The Canadians fortunately managed to avoid drawing the United States in preliminary pool play, but the team's round-robin games would be difficult nonetheless. Canada opened the Olympics by meeting host Australia, with the prospect of also facing Yugoslavia and Russia in the first round.

Steve had always dreamed about being part of the Olympics. He had been bitterly disappointed in 1995 when he and the Canadian team had fallen one game short of qualifying for the 1996 Atlanta Games. Now that he had his ticket punched to Sydney, he was determined to make the most of the opportunity.

Steve was also determined that his Canadian teammates would enjoy the experience. While the team played some pre-Olympic exhibitions in Hong Kong prior to reaching Sydney, he anonymously donated $3,000 to each of his teammates through the coaching staff so that they could enjoy some pre-Games shopping. And on the seventeen-hour flight overseas, he surrendered the first-class ticket provided to him by Canada Basketball—a contractual requirement for all NBA players heading to international competitions—telling Triano to give it to one of the taller players on the team who really needed the legroom.

As the national team centralized in July and toured for its pre-Olympic training and exhibitions, Steve shared a hotel room with teammate Andrew Mavis, getting some guitar lessons from his teammate and fellow B.C. native while he was at it.

Triano, the Canadian head coach, whom Steve had known since he was a teenager, was pleased to see his best player also prove to be the team's hardest worker. Despite being an NBA regular with a huge contract, Steve often led the team's drills, and Triano described him as Canada's best defender.

Steve had known many of his Olympic teammates since he was seventeen, when, as an eleventh-grade standout, he had been invited to try out for the Canadian Junior team for the 1991 World Championships in Edmonton. He had been cut from that squad but served as an alternate. "I was skinny, weak, and slow," Nash would later admit. Nine years later, Steve found himself the focal point of the Canadian team, trying to medal at the Olympics for the first time since 1936, when Canada captured silver in the Games' inaugural men's basketball competition at Berlin.

"We want the ball in Steve's hands," Triano told reporters as the Games opened in Australia. "He makes good decisions. He finds the open man. He's our leader and we want him to have the ball."

Steve felt a tremendous bond with teammates such as Rowan Barrett, Michael Meeks, and Todd MacCulloch, a seven-footer from Winnipeg and the only other NBA player on the Canadian roster. He felt an overwhelming pride in playing for his country on the world's grandest sporting stage. As Steve marched with the rest of the 309-member Canadian team into Stadium Australia for the opening ceremony on September 15, 2000, he had already accomplished a lifelong goal.

For Steve, the Olympics represented the ideal of sport that had captured his imagination as a youngster. The NBA, in comparison, was all business. At Sydney, he wasn't playing for money. He was playing for Canada, because he loved his country and wanted to represent it to the best of his abilities.

"Before I even played basketball at all, the Olympics were a big dream for me, no matter what sport I was thinking of," Steve confided before the Sydney Games. "So this is a dream come true. It's actually great for me to be here because I love the guys on this team."

Not content to merely be at the Olympics, however, Steve and his teammates immediately began to fashion the feel-good story of the Games. In their preliminary round game against host Australia, an overwhelming favorite playing at home, Steve burst out of the gates with a 15-point, 15-assist performance and Canada stunned the Aussies 101–90. The upstart Canadians continued their impressive run through the preliminary round, finishing with a 4–1 record including easy wins over Spain and Angola. Their only loss came against Russia.

Although the victory over Australia was impressive, Steve and his teammates also set the basketball world on its ear with a shocking 83–75 upset over defending World Champion Yugoslavia in their final game of the round-robin. Yugoslavia had been considered a co-favorite in the Olympic tournament along with the United States, and, in their most recent meeting with Canada two years earlier, they had won by a staggering margin of 45 points. Nobody had given Canada much of a chance in this game. But Steve scored 14 points over the final six minutes to help the Canadians overcome a 12-point deficit. Included in that clutch performance was a game-deciding basket with forty-seven seconds left that extended Canada's lead to 3 points and served as the knockout blow for the Yugoslavians. On that decisive play, Steve drove around a pick and toward the hoop before spinning in a pumping, left-handed hook shot over the outstretched arms of the Yugoslavian big men.

Steve would finish the Yugoslavia game with 26 points, 8 rebounds, 8 assists, 1 steal, and just 1 turnover. In the heat of the second half, he had scored 20 points and made all four three-pointers he attempted.

After the buzzer had sounded on what many were describing as the biggest victory in Canadian basketball history, Steve found himself wrapped in the arms of teammate Pete Guarasci, a powerful six-foot-nine forward, who carried the mop-topped "Captain Canada" around the court in celebration.

"Outside of all the skill and talent he possesses, he's got a heart—a heart that you rarely see in sports," Steve's teammate and good friend Rowan Barrett told reporters after the win. "And I think that typifies our whole team."

Steve referred to the victory over Yugoslavia as the game of his life. "For me, hopefully all the kids at home can really enjoy the win and be proud to be Canadian, and all the little basketball players can be proud to be Canadian basketball players because there's not always been that source of pride as far as Canada goes in basketball," he told reporters. "We've always been proud to be Canadian, now we can be proud to be Canadian basketball players and athletes."

That huge win sent Canada into the quarterfinals against France, which was considered by most to be an inferior team to Yugoslavia's. All Canada needed was a victory in that game to reach the semifinals and have a shot at the country's first men's basketball medal in sixty-four years.

But the French had been paying close attention to the Canadian run through the Olympic tournament. They were well aware that the key to stopping Canada was to limit the effectiveness of Steve Nash as much as possible. French coach Jean-Pierre DeVincenzi assigned Makan Dioumassi, a bigger, more physical guard, to dog Steve everywhere he went on the court. Dioumassi's game plan was obviously to be as physical as the referees would allow.

On this night, the officials gave the Frenchman wide latitude as he jostled Steve up and down the court from the opening tip. The result was Nash's worst game of the tournament. Steve got very few open looks at the basket and he was constantly being bumped and pushed by Dioumassi.

Steve finished the game with just 10 points and 1 rebound. He had 8 assists, but the French defense had also forced him into 9 turnovers. Meanwhile, nobody else on the Canadian team had stepped up sufficiently to make the difference. France won the game 68–63, ending Canada's chances at an Olympic medal.

The Canadians' run was over, and Steve didn't know whether he would ever play in the Olympics or with these special teammates again. He was bitterly disappointed, especially since he believed that, on most days, his Canadian team would have beaten France. As he left the court, Steve couldn't hold back the tears.

During the post-game media session, Canadian coach Jay Triano gave the French credit for their strategy. If anybody understood the vagaries of international basketball and the fluctuation in the way such games are officiated it was Triano, a former captain of the national team who had guided Canada to a sixth-place finish at the Seoul Olympics in 1988 and a fourth-place showing at the 1984 Los Angeles Games.

"If they don't blow the whistle, he's successful," Triano said of Dioumassi's defense on Nash. "If they blow it, Steve shoots fifteen foul shots. That's international basketball—you never know. Sometimes they call the hand check, sometimes they don't. Tonight, they didn't call it."

Seeing their dreams so close, only to end in disappointment, was too much for Steve to take. "When I looked at my teammates and saw that we were walking off the court unsuccessful it was very difficult to handle," he would tell the Canadian Press in the ensuing weeks. "I'll never forget the loss. There'll always be a bit of disappointment."

Steve Nash and the Canadians had to quickly swallow their disappointment and get ready to face Russia in a game to decide seventh-place in the Olympic tournament. It would have been easy for another team to let that game slide, but not this group. They had come too far together to go out with a whimper.

Although the lay-up that would have beaten the Russians at the end of the first overtime came a fraction of a second too late, Steve made up for it in the second extra session. He scored 6 straight points as Canada beat Russia 86–83 in double overtime. Canada had overcome a 7-point halftime deficit to force the extra periods.

The win gave Canada a seventh-place finish in the Olympics, far higher than most would have predicted for a team that many had said would never make it to Australia in the first place. The Canadians finished the Olympic tournament with a 5–2 record, the second best in the entire field. Their second loss had simply come at the wrong time, but they had gained the respect of the international basketball community during their Sydney run.

Steve Nash had also gained respect from those Canadians back home who weren't hard-core basketball fans, and from hoops followers worldwide who hadn't yet seen these types of performances regularly from him in the NBA.

"I just wanted to see all my teammates and coaches get a medal and step on the podium," Nash told reporters upon arriving back at Vancouver International Airport following the Olympics. "I'm really proud to be a part of this team. I wish everyone had the chance to be part of a group like this at some point in their lives."

In the summer of 2003, Steve Nash pulled on a Canadian jersey once again. In what would probably be his final tour with the national team, he led many of the same players who had played so well in Sydney in an attempt to qualify for the 2004 Athens Olympics.

Once again, the qualifying Tournament of the Americas was a ten-day grind in San Juan, Puerto Rico. But this time, fate wasn't as kind to the Canadian team.

A rare foot ailment that would ultimately end the NBA career of center Todd MacCulloch kept the seven-footer out of this qualifying event, leaving Steve as the only NBA player on the squad. And although he turned in another sterling effort, it wasn't enough for Canada to qualify for the 2004 Olympics.

Canada did come close, however. With Steve scoring 17 points and adding 7 assists and 9 rebounds, the team beat host Puerto Rico 89–79 in the first round. Steve also finished with a sterling 24 points and 10 assists, hitting all six of his three-point attempts, as Canada fell 94–90 to the defending World silver medalist Argentineans.

Wins over Brazil and the Dominican Republic qualified Canada for the semifinals, leaving Steve and his teammates two chances to gain a berth in the Athens Olympics. But that would prove frustratingly elusive. Canada fell 88–72 to Argentina in a semifinal blowout, then lost 79–66 to host Puerto Rico in the third-place game.

The tournament ended on a frustrating note for Steve, who went just 2-for-13 from the field in the loss to Puerto Rico, which avenged its crushing home-court defeat to Canada in the 1999 Olympic qualifying tournament. Nevertheless, Steve was named the tournament's Most Valuable Player once again, beating runner-up Manu Ginobili of the San Antonio Spurs, who starred for Argentina, and third-place finisher Tim Duncan of the United States, Ginobli's San Antonio teammate.

Reflecting on it now, Steve cherishes his time wearing the red and white for Canada, particularly his Olympic experience in Sydney alongside a bunch of teammates he considers lifelong friends. "It was amazing. It was one of the best experiences of my career. It may be *the* best experience of my career, I don't know," he says now.

"First of all, the Olympics speak for themselves. They are one of those great parts of sports. It was something I always really, really wanted to be a part of.

"Second, for us to really enjoy each other and to have such a closeness and so much chemistry and history together, that just topped it all off. That was extremely special for us and I thought we played like it."

Steve Nash has been an important figure for Canadian basketball since the early 1990s. While other Canadian NBA players such as Rick Fox and Jamaal Magloire have often shown reluctance to give up their free time to represent the country internationally, Steve has routinely surrendered his off-seasons to wear the Maple Leaf, playing in ten of twelve summers between 1991 and 2003. Steve values the time spent representing Canada and recognizes that it has played an important role in his development as a player. Following the 2000 Olympic tournament, he even tried to switch his NBA uniform number in Dallas from 13 to 7, the number he wore for Canada in the Sydney Olympics. The NBA refused to allow the switch for merchandising reasons.

"You go into another country and you're wearing that name across your chest and you feel like you really are representing the whole country," he says. "I'm definitely 100 percent proud of being Canadian. I love Canada."

11

A TURNING POINT

"There are a lot of great players in this league, but to be put in the upper group was something I always expected of myself."

—Steve Nash, first-time NBA All-Star, 2002

As Steve Nash returned to North America from the Sydney Olympics, he was exhausted. At this point, between the NBA and his international games, he had been playing basketball for nearly two straight years without a significant break. And just a couple of days after his final Olympic appearance in Australia, he was already back into the regular two-a-day workout grind of another training camp with the Dallas Mavericks.

But despite the fatigue, Steve was also excited about the season that lay ahead. He sensed that both he and the Mavericks were ready to turn a corner.

Although injuries had continued to plague him during his second season in Dallas, limiting Steve to fifty-six games, things had been generally more positive with the

Mavericks. He hadn't been booed again by his team's own fans, for starters. He had made nearly 48 percent of his shots, compared to the dismal 36 percent of the previous season. And he had raised his scoring average to 8.6 points, with 4.9 assists, per game.

These numbers were still far short of what Dallas fans and management had been hoping for, though, and Steve had even been supplanted for a time by Robert Pack as the Mavericks' starting point guard. "Dallas fans are not sold on the Mavericks," Steve had told a friend early in the 1999–2000 season. "I think a lot of them aren't sold on me, to be honest, but that's up to them."

Still, the Mavericks had posted a 31–19 record from early January 2000 on, after dot-com billionaire Mark Cuban purchased the team from former owner Ross Perot, Jr. The team had finished the season with a 40–42 mark, barely missing a playoff spot. Dirk Nowitzki was beginning to develop into the sharpshooting star Don Nelson had predicted when the team plucked him as a teenager out of Germany, and Steve had enjoyed his finest stretch as a Maverick over the final ten games of the season. Now, after a spectacular Olympic performance by their point guard in Australia, Dallas basketball fans had great expectations as the 2000–2001 season dawned.

The fact that the Dallas turnaround had begun at the same time as Mark Cuban's purchase of the team was hardly a coincidence. Cuban was a rabid basketball fan who had been a Mavericks season-ticket-holder for many years. Now, after selling the Broadcast.com enterprise he had co-founded to Yahoo! for $5 billion, he had more than enough resources to purchase his own franchise. Cuban eagerly dived into his new role as owner, doing his utmost to make Dallas an appealing place for NBA players after years of the franchise being regarded as one of the league's least desirable destinations.

Cuban brought a new standard to the Dallas organization, providing his players with a luxurious locker room—complete with individual fourteen-inch flat-screen monitors, DVD players, satellite hookups, video games, stereo systems, and VCRs at each stall—a state-of-the-art weight and training facility, and even comfortable, high-backed chairs with recline and massage options on the home bench during games. The team traveled in style on a well-equipped private jet, and Cuban even sent a car service to players' homes to pick them up for a game when a rare snowstorm hit Dallas.

When Steve arrived at Vancouver International Airport after his adventure at the Olympics, he discovered that Cuban had sent his private plane to fly his point guard down to Dallas. It was typical of the lengths to which the owner was now willing to go to make his players feel comfortable and prepared.

While there was now terrific support from ownership in Dallas, however, there was still unmistakable pressure on Steve to perform. In fact, Cuban had put the heat directly on Nash prior to the Olympics by obtaining point guard Howard Eisley from the Utah Jazz. Eisley was seen as an up-and-comer in NBA circles after he'd capably backed up legend John Stockton for a contending team in Utah. When Cuban's management signed Eisley to a seven-year, US$41-million deal in July, it sent a clear message to Steve Nash that he would have some serious competition in camp.

That fact didn't trouble Steve. By now, he had become accustomed to the concept of fighting for a job. Of much greater concern was fatigue. He only hoped he could stay energetic and avoid injuries over the long grind of the NBA season after the summer-long Olympic effort.

"I think I'm ready to have sort of a defining year for me in the NBA," he confided during training camp. "But it's going to be the most difficult year of my career."

As it turned out, it would also be the best season of Steve's NBA career to that point—the year he would break through as a legitimate starter and impact player in the league. In his fifth pro season, everything came together for the twenty-six-year-old Canadian as he averaged 15.6 points—nearly twice his previous best in Dallas—as well as career highs of 7.3 assists and 3.2 rebounds.

"He really put that [Canadian Olympic] team on his back and that confidence has just followed right through training camp," Mavericks assistant coach Donnie Nelson told the Fort Worth *Star-Telegram* early in that season. "We're seeing the guy that we made the Phoenix trade for."

After an Olympics where he shouldered much of the scoring load for Canada, Steve stepped up as an offensive threat for the Mavericks in 2000–2001 as well, attempting over two hundred shots more than he had taken in any prior NBA season and hitting nearly half of them.

Despite the back-breaking schedule, Steve also managed to play seventy games during that NBA regular season. Most importantly, his on-court leadership helped the Mavericks continue to blossom as a team. Dallas rolled up a 53–29 record, a thirteen-game improvement over the previous regular season, to make the playoffs for the first time in eleven years.

"I don't think it was a turning point just because of the Olympics, but it was at a point in my career where I had come back from the injuries and really trained hard and started to feel great again," Steve says now, reflecting on that benchmark season. "It basically was the point where I picked up where I'd left off after my second year [in Phoenix]. It wasn't that Olympic experience that necessarily put me over the top. I think I'd worked really hard to play well in Sydney, but it was the culmination of my health and hard work."

Steve also showed previously skeptical Mavericks fans something extra during the playoffs of 2001, the first post-season appearance for the Dallas franchise since 1990. After falling behind 2–0 to the veteran-laden Utah Jazz in their first-round series, the Mavericks bounced back to beat the Jazz in three straight games. In doing so, Dallas became only the sixth team in NBA history to overcome a 2–0 deficit in a post-season series.

Steve was instrumental in the victory over Utah. He pumped in 27 points to help Dallas stay alive in Game 4. Then, after suffering through a horrible 0-for-7 shooting start and a sprained ankle in Game 5, he nailed a trio of three-pointers in the fourth quarter as the Mavericks overcame a 17-point Utah lead to stun the Jazz and their fans 84–83.

"That game had to rate right up there for me," Steve said after the hard-fought series was over. "The Olympics were something totally different, for a lot of reasons. But this win was as big as any I've ever had in basketball. It was a lot of fun."

Steve and the Mavericks would go on to fall 4–1 to the San Antonio Spurs in the second round of those 2001 playoffs, but the season as a whole was considered a major breakthrough for both Nash and the Dallas organization. "I've noticed in the playoffs people really respecting me as a player and taking notice. That's very rewarding," Steve told a friend during the post-season run. "I've worked hard and wanted to be in this situation for a long time."

The 2000–2001 season was just the beginning of Steve Nash's ascension in Dallas. Over the next two years, his production and efficiency steadily climbed, and so did the Mavericks' fortunes. In 2001–2002, the team finished with a 57–25 record, almost a mirror image of the club's sorry state when Steve had arrived in Dallas three years earlier. During that season, he upped his personal averages to 17.9 points and 7.7 assists per game while steering Dallas to the league's highest-scoring offense. Impressively, Steve also helped Dallas finish with the fewest turnovers in the league.

Steve truly arrived as one of the NBA's premier players that season, cracking the All-NBA Third Team at year's end and helping the Mavericks again reach the second round of the playoffs. The player who three years earlier had nearly been booed out of Reunion Arena had now become the shaggy-haired darling of Dallas fans. His efforts were rewarded with a mid-season selection to play alongside teammate Dirk Nowitzki for the Don Nelson–coached Western Conference team in the 2002 NBA All-Star Game at the First Union Center in Philadelphia.

"There are a lot of great players in this league, but to be put in the upper group was something I always expected of myself," Steve told a New York reporter prior to his first All-Star Game appearance. "Whether I get there and stay there is another thing, but it's something I believe I can do."

Steve Nash was in great spirits on February 7, 2002, as he and the Dallas Mavericks headed into the NBA All-Star break. The night before, the Mavericks had beaten the New Jersey Nets 112–100 at the Meadowlands, and tonight his teammates were taking him out in Manhattan to mark his twenty-eighth birthday before departing for the All-Star festivities in Philadelphia. It felt terrific for Steve to be among the NBA's elite after the shaky start he'd experienced in Dallas. Little did he know that this particular evening would have a far greater impact on his life than any All-Star Game selection.

While celebrating his birthday at a New York night-club, Steve couldn't help but notice the striking dark-haired woman serving drinks to his group. He struck up a conversation with the waitress and discovered she was from Paraguay but had lived in the city for three years, and that she was studying to become a personal fitness trainer. Her named was Alejandra Amarilla.

Sometime during the evening, Steve told her that he and his friends played basketball. She didn't recognize him as an NBA star. "Oh, yeah, I work out too," she replied.

Intrigued, Steve asked Alejandra for her phone number before his group left the nightclub. They hadn't had a chance to talk all that much, but Steve was determined to get to know this woman better.

"I really was hoping I'd get to know her and I just squeaked her number out of her at the end of the night. But, who knows, right? It's a different city and I'd barely ever talked to her. But I definitely was extremely interested," Steve says now.

"We stayed in touch and started kind of building a friendship on the phone. And I came to New York that summer and I didn't know what to expect. We spent every day together. So, from then on ..."

From then on, the two were a couple, with Steve spending much of the NBA off-seasons in New York, where the majority of Alejandra's friends and family in North America were based. When the following NBA season began in the fall of 2002, Alejandra moved to Dallas to spend the winters with Steve.

"She's beautiful and she's really tough and honest and, you know, she's really amazing," Steve says now, describing the attraction. "We're opposites in a lot of ways. She's really organized and I'm not. She's really honest, to the point of confrontation, whereas I am very laid-back. So, I think in that way we're a pain in the ass for each other but very good for each other."

What made the situation in Dallas even more ideal for Steve during that 2001–2002 season was the fact that one of his longtime friends, a former basketball teammate from Victoria, had joined the staff of the Mavericks. Al Whitley and Steve had known each other since they were seven-year-olds. Whitley had been visiting Steve in Dallas, became friends with Mavericks owner Mark Cuban, and, before long, was offered a job in communications for the NBA team.

"I was kind of at a dead end and Mark asked me if I would be interested in coming to work for the Mavericks in Dallas, and, of course, I jumped at the opportunity," Whitley says now.

A year later, he had moved over to the basketball operations side of the business, and before long he was the head equipment manager. So while Steve was tearing up the league for Dallas, one of his best childhood friends was making sure he and all his teammates were taken care of in the locker room. For Whitley, a former Canadian university player and basketball junkie, the opportunity to travel with the Mavericks and be part of an NBA team was the break of a lifetime.

Steve's finest season in a Dallas uniform came in 2002–2003, when he led the Mavericks into the NBA's Western Conference finals for only the second time in franchise history. That impressive playoff run came after

Dallas had finished with 60 wins and 22 losses in the regular season, the best record ever for the Mavericks.

Once again, Steve turned in fine regular-season numbers, scoring 17.7 points per game and adding 7.3 assists per contest. He also hit a franchise-record forty-nine consecutive free throws during one stretch of that campaign.

He and Dirk Nowitzki were again selected to play in the NBA's mid-season classic. "I just love the fact that we can go play in the All-Star Game together," Steve told Canadian Press. "We've come from the bottom and worked our way up pretty high now, so we're trying to just continue to get better and give our team a chance to win a championship."

It was during this season that the Mavericks' "Big Three" truly emerged as a star force in the league, with Nash, Nowitzki, and Michael Finley combining to share Player-of-the-Month honors in November as the Mavericks got off to a franchise-best 14–0 start. The three were each able to post terrific statistics and share the basketball without the clash of egos found on many NBA teams. When Finley wasn't selected to play in the All-Star Game that February in Atlanta, Steve and Dirk wrote "FIN 4" on their basketball shoes in his honor.

Basketball was never hotter in Dallas than during the 2002–2003 season, when the Mavericks managed forty-one consecutive sell-outs in their new arena. Steve once again thrilled the home crowds by steering the Mavericks simultaneously to the league's highest-scoring offense and the NBA's fewest turnovers. The Nash-Nowitzki combination was one of the league's best, with Steve making the All-NBA Third Team and Dirk the Second Team at season's end.

For the first time in fifteen years, the Mavericks also put together a deep playoff run. But they did it the hard way, reaching the Western Conference finals by winning back-to-back Game 7s during the preliminary rounds.

In the opening round, the Mavericks jumped out to a 3–0 lead on Portland, before allowing the Trail Blazers to roar back and tie the series 3–3. In Game 4 of that series in Portland, Steve failed to score a single point and he had only 7 points in Game 5.

Despite the Mavericks' precarious situation and his own inconsistency early in the series, Steve was confident heading into Game 7, telling reporters, "I think we just need to believe. There is no question in my mind we can win that game."

He was right. In Game 7 at Dallas, Dirk Nowitzki bounced back from a 4-point effort the previous game to score 31. Steve added 21 points as the Mavericks won 107–95 to advance to the Western Conference semifinals.

The Mavericks put themselves in a quick hole to begin that series, though, falling 124–113 on home court to the Sacramento Kings. Despite scoring 20 points and adding 7 assists, Steve was angry after the loss. "We got embarrassed," he told reporters. "We can't play the way we played tonight and expect to win any game in this series."

Dallas rebounded to take the next two games, including a 141–137 double-overtime victory in Game 3 at Sacramento in which Steve led the way with 31 points.

But in Game 4 at Arco Arena, the Kings roared back to even the series at 2–2 with a 99–83 win, limiting Nash to 6 points.

The teams split the next two games to even the series at 3–3, setting up the second Game 7 for the Mavericks in as many series. Thanks to Dallas's regular-season record, the Mavericks enjoyed home-court advantage, and they made the most of it, pounding Sacramento 112–99 in front of more than 20,000 delirious fans. Steve contributed 18 points and 13 assists and dominated his Kings counterpart Mike Bibby in the key early stages as Dallas advanced to the Western Conference finals for the first time since 1988.

The next round began well for Steve and the Mavericks, as they stunned the home-court Spurs 113–110 in the series opener at San Antonio. Steve scored 22 points and Dirk Nowitzki led the way with 38 as Dallas hit forty-nine free throws to overcome an 18-point deficit and post the win.

But the Spurs, led by veteran big man Tim Duncan, Argentinean Manu Ginobili, and French point guard Tony Parker, bounced back to win the next three games of the series. Dirk Nowitzki suffered a strained left knee in Game 3 and was lost for the rest of the playoffs. With a 3–1 lead and Game 5 scheduled for San Antonio, it appeared as if the Spurs would easily close out the series at home.

Steve and his Maverick teammates weren't ready to surrender, however. Michael Finley scored 31 points and Steve added 14, including 7 in the decisive fourth quarter, as plucky Dallas beat the Spurs 103–91 in Game 5 by coming back from a 19-point first-half deficit.

"We feel as though anything is possible," Steve told reporters before Game 6 in Dallas. "If we just stay with it and allow ourselves to be in the game, we've got enough guys with the toughness to come through. We know our season could be over tomorrow night. At the same time, we feel real confident that we can push it to seven games, and in a seventh game we've been there before."

It wouldn't get that far, however. In Game 6 at Dallas, the Spurs showed their championship mettle, digging their way out of a 15-point hole late in the third quarter to beat the Mavericks 90–78. Thirty-seven-year-old Steve Kerr was the difference, as the veteran guard hit four three-pointers down the stretch to spark a 23–0 San Antonio run. Steve Nash was held to 6 points but managed 11 assists.

Despite the loss, the appreciative Dallas fans rose to their feet to applaud their team. In just four years, the Mavericks had transformed themselves from league doormats to NBA playoff semifinalists. And despite his personal disappointment with the outcome, Steve walked to center court and made a slow turn, applauding fans in all directions at the American Airlines Center.

"We have a lot to be proud of. At the same time, we didn't reach our goal, so it hurts," Steve told reporters. "We were so close to going to the finals. To not reach it is difficult to swallow."

Steve Nash and the Mavericks' meteoric rise through the ranks of the NBA would plateau slightly during the

2003–2004 season. Prior to that campaign, team management made several changes to the roster, bringing in All-Star forwards Antawn Jamison from Golden State and Antoine Walker from Boston. Suddenly, the high-octane Mavericks had so much firepower it was difficult to see how one basketball could possibly satisfy the shooting desires of the entire crew.

The Mavericks had actually tried to land a legitimate center by signing veteran free agent Alonzo Mourning. But after Mourning opted to join New Jersey instead, Dallas's Plan B was simply to add more firepower to the league's highest-scoring roster. They shipped Nick Van Exel to Golden State in exchange for Jamison and tough forward Danny Fortson in August. But they weren't finished there. In the middle of training camp, the Mavericks acquired Antoine Walker and point guard Tony Delk from the Boston Celtics in exchange for forward Raef LaFrentz.

"We've been able to add a lot of guys who can do a lot of different things and make a really dynamic lineup," Steve told reporters as the season dawned. "I think it's a beautiful thing. We're going to be a great team to watch and hopefully an even better team on the floor…. There are enough shots to go around."

In Jamison and Walker, the Mavericks were adding two players who had each averaged better than 20 points per game the previous season to the already considerable "Big Three" of Dirk Nowitzki, Steve Nash, and Michael Finley. The job of trying to ensure that everybody got enough touches fell to Steve, who passed up many of his own opportunities early on to try to keep all of his team-mates involved and happy. As a result, Steve's scoring average fell to 14.5 points per game in 2003–2004, more than 3 points lower than the previous season. Although his assists rose slightly, to 8.8 per game, some saw the scoring drop as a warning sign that a thirty-year-old Nash could no longer be expected to handle the rigors of an eighty-two-game NBA schedule.

Perhaps that was why the Mavericks took no action to extend Steve's contract as that season progressed, even though he was scheduled to become a free agent on July 1, 2004. As the season continued, Steve was mildly disap-pointed at the lack of an offer, but he still firmly believed he would remain a Maverick. He felt he had played extremely well over the final two-thirds of the 2003–2004 season, as Dallas rolled up a franchise-best 36–5 record at home and a 52–30 mark overall.

But the year ended with a disappointing loss to the Sacramento Kings in a best-of-seven first-round playoff series, during which Steve was out-dueled by Kings point guard Mike Bibby.

Sacramento jumped on the Mavericks early, winning the first two games of the series at home. The Kings enjoyed the home-court advantage primarily because Dallas hadn't been able to win consistently on the road during the 2003–2004 season. After recording the league's best road record the previous year, the Mavericks had been just 16–25 away from home.

The Mavericks found themselves in a 2–0 hole after losing 83–79 in Sacramento in Game 2. Bibby scored

24 points in that game, including 10 in the final quarter. Meanwhile, Steve missed a key three-pointer with nineteen seconds left.

After bouncing back to win Game 3 in Dallas by 25 points, the Mavericks looked as though they would make it a series. But they fell into a 3–1 hole by losing Game 4 at home by a 94–92 margin when Steve missed an eighteen-foot jumper with just over eight seconds remaining.

Back in Sacramento, the Kings smelled blood and wrapped up the series with a 119–118 thriller in Arco Arena. Dirk Nowitzki's jumper at the buzzer that would have won it for the Mavericks caught front-iron. Mike Bibby put a cap on a terrific series by nailing six three-pointers and scoring 36 points.

Steve also had a strong game with 24 points, 14 assists, and 7 rebounds. But the Associated Press reported that Steve had a "miserable series against Sacramento until the finale, and even then was outplayed by Mike Bibby." TV commentators echoed that sentiment. The strong showing by Bibby seemed to fuel talk about whether Steve's now thirty-year-old body could stand up for an entire regular season and playoff run.

"It was just a really slow start to that season because we had a whole new team and I was always trying to incorporate everyone and make it work before I looked for my own success," Steve says now. "But I knew I was going to get better and better still and I was extremely motivated to make up for a disappointing year as a team."

12

HERE COME THE SUNS

"I thought it was a no-brainer for me to come back to Dallas.... It was interesting for it all to change so fast."
—Steve Nash, returning to Phoenix, July 2004

The clock had barely ticked past 11:00 p.m. when Bill Duffy's cell phone began to ring. Less than a minute into the NBA's 2004 free-agent negotiation period and the Phoenix Suns were already calling. They were interested in Duffy's longtime client, point guard Steve Nash.

Steve was sitting in his Dallas home, beside Duffy, when the call came in. Since he had decided to opt out of the final year of his contract with the Mavericks and test the free-agent market, both he and his agent had expected there would be some immediate interest. Suns president Bryan Colangelo was first off the mark, just seconds past the midnight (Eastern Daylight Time) league deadline after which teams could begin talking to free agents.

"I want to be the first to call, to let you know how interested we are in Steve," the Suns boss told Duffy,

Steve's agent and close friend ever since the end of his senior year at Santa Clara. "We think this is where he should be, and I just want to make that real clear to Steve."

Duffy handed the phone to his client. The Suns' full-court press for Steve Nash had officially begun.

Steve had just returned from six weeks in Europe and England, but he had already been tipped off by Duffy that the Suns were interested and were preparing to make an offer. At that moment, however, Steve didn't think he was going to be playing basketball anywhere other than Dallas. He had become a two-time NBA All-Star there and, along with Dirk Nowitzki and Michael Finley, had transformed the Mavericks from one of the worst teams in the league into one of the best. After initially struggling to find his way in Dallas, Steve now saw himself finishing his basketball career in Texas.

But the Mavericks had not taken immediate steps to lock up Steve's services for the long term. While they had signed both Finley and Nowitzki to big-money contract extensions, they had almost indifferently allowed Nash to become a free agent. Despite being one of the top three players on the team and the key to the Mavericks' high-octane offense, Steve had been only Dallas's sixth-highest-paid player in 2003–2004, and his contract for the next season, if he stayed put, would keep him at US$5.75 million. It was terrific money, but it wasn't close to what other NBA All-Stars were earning. That troubled Steve to a certain degree. He felt he had been a big part of the Mavericks' turnaround, and the fact that the team was not proactively making moves to keep him was disappointing.

It was widely assumed in NBA circles that the Mavericks would simply wait to see what offers came Steve's way and match the best of them. The team had even said as much publicly. "Steve doesn't want to leave and we have the financial means to keep him…. It should not be a problem," Dallas coach and general manager Don Nelson had told reporters after the team was eliminated in the first round of the 2004 playoffs.

Steve was also intent on staying in Texas and had said so several times. He and his partner, Alejandra, were expecting twins that fall. He felt established in Dallas. The fans who had booed him just a few years earlier now fiercely supported him. With his good friend Dirk Nowitzki emerging as a dominant NBA forward, and a solid core of young talent surrounding them, Steve felt the Mavericks had a legitimate shot at winning a championship.

"If the Mavs came to me today with an offer I couldn't refuse, it'd be over, because this is where I really want to be," Steve told reporters in Dallas. "It's important to me to try everything I can do to be here." But since Dallas had yet to make a move, he and Duffy now thought it was only prudent to at least listen to offers from other teams. "It would be nice if they valued me enough that we didn't have to go that route," Steve told reporters. "If it comes down to having to entertain other offers, that's part of the game as well. I'm prepared to do that."

Steve was mildly surprised but not shocked to hear that the Suns were interested in reacquiring him. He had maintained a good relationship with Bryan and Jerry Colangelo after leaving Phoenix following his second NBA season. He had a lot of respect for the people in the Suns organization, one of the league's model franchises, and he believed the feeling was mutual. He also knew the Suns were now looking for an experienced point guard to steer an athletic, talented young group of players. Just a few months earlier, they had traded away Stephon Marbury to the New York Knicks, clearing significant room under their team salary cap. Phoenix certainly had the means to pay a top-caliber point guard.

A few minutes after Bryan Colangelo's call, the phone at Steve's house rang again. It was Rex Chapman, a former teammate with the Suns and a good friend who was now a scout for Phoenix. Despite the late hour—just forty-five minutes before midnight, Dallas time—Chapman asked if he could pop by for a few minutes.

Chapman was one of the veterans who had helped Steve ease into the NBA as a rookie with Phoenix during the 1996–97 season. The two old friends sat up late into the night catching up, with Chapman also trying to gauge whether Steve would consider making a move at this stage of his career. Chapman also brought along a gift—a ninety-six-page book that the Suns had printed for the sole purpose of using it in their recruiting pitch to Steve.

On the cover of the large, black, leather-bound publication were the Suns logo and the title, *Turning*

Point. Inside were details of the franchise's plan to rebuild, from the team that had missed the playoffs the previous spring with a 29–53 record into a championship contender. The book included information about the Suns' young stars Amare Stoudemire, NBA Rookie of the Year in 2002–2003, and Shawn Marion, the high-flying forward whom the Suns had drafted with a pick obtained when they traded Steve to Dallas in 1998. The book even featured several pictures of Steve digitally altered to show him wearing a Suns number 13 uniform, illustrating how he would fit in as the leader and central piece of their rebuilding project. Finally, it showed his picture in the Suns' Ring of Honor, dedicated to the greatest players in franchise history, whose numbers are retired.

While Steve had known there would be some interest in him as a free agent, the Suns' enthusiasm was already blowing him away.

Before going to bed that evening, Steve received calls from both the Mavericks and the Suns, saying they would like to meet with him the next morning. As he awoke on July 1, however, he was unaware that an impressive Suns recruiting party was already mustering at the Deer Valley Airport just outside Phoenix. At 7:00 a.m., the Suns' new controlling owner, Robert Sarver, had boarded his Canadair Challenger jet, along with Jerry and Bryan Colangelo; Phoenix head coach Mike D'Antoni; minority owner, consultant, and former Suns player Steve Kerr; and star forward Amare Stoudemire. There was only one reason for this early-morning flight to Dallas and just one prize with which this group aimed to return to the desert—Steve Nash.

As the Suns contingent touched down in Dallas, Steve and Bill Duffy were already talking to the Mavericks, but things weren't going well. Dallas general manager Donnie Nelson had no firm salary offer for Steve, who thought the team was handling his situation very sloppily. Nelson told Steve that billionaire owner Mark Cuban hadn't given him authorization to negotiate.

"So why don't we get Mark over here, because we're going to be meeting with other teams?" Steve suggested to Nelson, feeling as though this exercise with the Mavericks was quickly turning into a waste of time. When Cuban did arrive, Steve got the distinct impression that the Dallas owner didn't feel Steve's contract situation was particularly important. He sensed no urgency on Cuban's part. "It seemed like he didn't want me back, really," Steve says now, describing the meeting.

As the session with Cuban ended, Steve felt discouraged. It hurt that he had put so much hard work into helping turn things around in Dallas only to sense indifference from the owner when it came to keeping him on the team. Steve had fully expected Cuban to make an offer in the ballpark of what other NBA teams would be presenting, but so far, Dallas hadn't even made a formal proposal. And the money they were loosely pitching—four years at US$36-million—was well below what he and Duffy knew would be offered elsewhere. It became obvious to Steve during that meeting that he would now have to look seriously at other teams.

About an hour after Steve met with Cuban, the Phoenix contingent sent a car service to bring Nash and Duffy to the lavish Dallas home of John Landon, who had become a minority owner in the Suns franchise that summer. Landon's house would become the Suns' head-quarters in a day-long sales pitch aimed at repatriating their former point guard.

As he and Duffy arrived at the large house, Steve was surprised at the size and caliber of the Suns' contingent. Seeing the team's new owner there to personally recruit him, along with senior management, the head coach, and the Suns' young superstar, made him feel wanted. Regardless of what would transpire that day, Steve already felt appreciated and deeply honored by the gesture. It was certainly a much more positive feeling than the one he had got from Dallas.

After lunch, the Phoenix group began its sales pitch to Steve, with each person telling him how he could be the key in their chase for a championship. They wanted his leader-ship and veteran toughness to help mold their young team into a championship contender. When Amare Stoudemire was asked to speak, Steve was impressed by the bluntness of the power forward's message—that Steve's leadership and passing skills were precisely what the talented young group assembled in Phoenix required in order to take the next step. "Look, I need you," Stoudemire began.

Steve listened as the Colangelos spelled out the financial terms of the Phoenix offer. The numbers were staggering. The Suns were willing to put up US$65 million over a six-year deal to lure him back to Arizona. At nearly US$11 million a season, that was almost double what he was scheduled to make in Dallas for the coming season, and far above anything the Mavericks had talked about for a future contract.

Steve and Bill Duffy excused themselves from the Phoenix group and huddled in the massive media room of the luxurious house. By this time, Steve was feeling seriously torn. He felt a deep loyalty to the Dallas teammates with whom he had already come so far. But at the same time, the enthusiasm the Suns were showing was astounding, and far beyond any interest he was feeling from the Mavericks.

"I know your heart lies with Dallas," Duffy told Steve, "but you're a free agent now. You've got to look at every opportunity, and this looks like a pretty good one."

It certainly did. The money being offered was immense, but the length of the contract was also appealing to Steve, who had turned thirty years old that February. He was also impressed with the young core in Phoenix—Amare Stoudemire, Shawn Marion, Joe Johnson, and Leandro Barbosa. He knew these guys collectively had far more talent than their record the previous year indicated. There was nowhere to go in Phoenix but up. Perhaps most of all, it felt great to be so aggressively sought by the Suns.

But Steve felt obliged to give the Mavericks a chance to make a new pitch. He called Mark Cuban, but Cuban wasn't prepared to come close to the Suns' offer. The Dallas owner wanted to discuss the option of signing

Steve and then trading him to Phoenix. The Suns weren't interested in that scenario. The Phoenix contingent was also asking him for a quick decision. They didn't want to drag out their pursuit of Steve Nash past that day.

By this time, Steve felt the decision had practically been made for him. The Suns had put on a full-court press to regain his services. Their generous offer and all-out effort and enthusiasm felt good. Everything was happening so fast, but Steve was certain he was making the right move.

As he and Bill Duffy walked through the door of the home theater and into the room where the Suns party was waiting, Steve knew he was stepping into a new era for himself and his family. "Okay, I'm a Phoenix Sun!" He smiled at the group that had been sitting nervously on the other side.

Nash and Jerry Colangelo hugged. Amare Stoudemire rubbed his hands together. Somebody opened a bottle of Champagne and the group gathered for a toast.

Steve shook hands on the deal with Jerry Colangelo, the same man who eight years earlier had made the draft pick to bring him into the NBA. Under league rules, the contract couldn't officially be signed until two weeks later, but that was just a formality. He had done it. He was headed back to Phoenix.

Steve was in the car returning home when he called Michael Finley and Dirk Nowitzki to break the news to his Dallas teammates. This part was tough. Finley couldn't believe that the Mavericks hadn't done more to keep their point guard. Nowitzki realized Steve had made the right decision. "You gotta go," Dirk told him. "That's a great deal."

In one day, his entire future in the NBA had taken a new and surprising direction. Steve would be embarking on another major rebuilding project. He didn't know what lay ahead but he was sure of one thing—the Suns wanted him to be part of it. *It feels great to go somewhere I'm really wanted,* he thought.

"I just didn't know it would come to that," Steve says now, reflecting on the biggest move of his career. "I thought that Mark would make an offer in the ballpark and I would stay in Dallas. And really, for me, looking back, he didn't want me back at all. You know, he tries to spin it to say that I left for the money or whatever it was, but he didn't value me. He never really made an offer. He floated around a four-year and $36-million deal. That's almost $30 million short. So to me, it just says he never planned on having me back."

Mavericks coach and general manager Don Nelson took the news hard. "I never dreamed we'd lose Nash or any other player of his magnitude," Nelson told the Associated Press when news of Steve's departure leaked out. "It's not like a trade, where you get something back…. We lost a big part of our team and we don't have anything to fill it. It's a setback." Nelson would step down as coach and general manager of the Mavericks near the end of the 2004–2005 season, making way for new coach Avery Johnson.

Meanwhile, Mark Cuban would defend his decision not to match the Suns' generous offer to Steve. On his much-read personal blog, the Mavericks owner said the fact that Nash had been able to play in all but four regular-season games for the Mavericks over the previous three years was "improbable." Cuban wrote that it would be "a matter of time before his style of play caught up with him."

Cuban's Mavericks used some of the salary-cap space freed up by Steve Nash's exit to pay center Erick Dampier beefing up the team in the middle. They also obtained speedy Jason Terry to replace Steve as the Dallas point guard.

Cuban declines when asked to comment on how Steve's departure from Dallas played out, saying he'll leave that to the player to explain. But he remembers feeling the wrath of Mavericks' fans when Steve's signing with Phoenix became public. "I took a ton of criticism. It's part of the business," Cuban says now. "I was sad to see Steve leave. But I have always respected his decision."

Steve believes that the questions around his durability weren't fair. Despite discovering after he joined the Suns that he had a congenital back problem that causes vertebrae to slip, he still managed to play back-to-back eighty-two-game seasons for the Mavericks and perform well in the majority of his playoff games for the team.

"I think that was ridiculous for people to make that claim," Steve says now of the theory that he was prone to wearing down over the course of a long season. "I think of all the point guards out there, I've got to be in the top percentage of games played. So I think it was always a stretch for people to come out and say that."

Nobody was more stunned to hear about Steve Nash leaving Dallas than Al Whitley. For the Mavericks' head equipment manager and Steve's childhood buddy, what transpired on July 1, 2004, was a wake-up call.

"You know, when Steve left Dallas it was really a huge lesson for me that the NBA is a business, first and foremost," Whitley says now. "And no matter what you do and how much you accomplish, at the end of the day it is a business and owners are writing these big checks and they've got to do what they feel is in the best interests of the team, and players have to do what's in the best interest of their families.

"It can get sticky," adds Whitley, who would one day like to be an NBA general manager. "At first I didn't really understand it. But now, as time's evolved and I've learned a lot more about the salary cap and all that stuff, Mark had to do what he had to do and, obviously, Steve got an unbelievable offer from Phoenix and it was a no-brainer taking that."

13

NEW ERA
IN NASH-VILLE

"I thought it would be a great fit. I was excited to try to take those guys and make them something better."

—Steve Nash, back in the desert, 2004

Returning to the Phoenix Suns was a major step for Steve Nash. But it was only the second-biggest event in the life of the thirty-year-old point guard during the fall of 2004.

On October 14 of that year, Alejandra and Steve became parents of twin girls, Lourdes and Isabella. Steve was in the operating room when the babies were born by cesarean section.

The girls arrived five weeks premature and had to spend a week in a Phoenix hospital—one in the neonatal intensive care unit, the other in intermediate care—before the couple could take them home. "It was difficult some days, but overall everyone felt really confident that they'd be fine," Steve says now.

The experience of being there for his children's birth is something Steve, along with thousands of other fathers, describes simply as "unbelievable."

"It was different for us," he says. "We had a C-section. It was different, but it was incredible. It was obviously a highlight of my life."

So much had changed for Steve and Alejandra over a four-month period. He was joining a new team, and the couple had purchased a new home in the Paradise Valley suburb of Phoenix—a 6,500-square-foot beauty with infinity pool, backyard gazebo, artificial putting green, and practice sand trap.

But the biggest change was that they now had a family of their own to look after. The arrival of the twins— nicknamed Lola and Bella—had transformed their lives forever.

"On one hand, it's just the greatest," Steve says of being a father. "It makes life more fun and it's just incredible— you can't really describe it. But on the other hand, it is more of a challenge, more of a responsibility, to balance everything. But I'm more than happy to do so. It's just so much fun to have two little girls that, you know, I'd sacrifice anything for."

Steve believes being a parent gives him an even greater reason to learn and try to become a better person every day. And despite his hectic schedule as a pro basketball player, he says he is fortunate to be able to spend a lot of time with his girls.

"I mean, you miss some things here and there, when you're on the road," he says. "But I'm also home a lot. You know, when I'm at home, I'm at home, not behind a desk. So I feel like I get a lot more time than a lot of people do with their kids."

Compounding the excitement in the Nash home during the fall of 2004 was Steve's big move to the Suns. He was joining a team that had gone 29–53 the previous season and missed the playoffs. Over the past few seasons, Phoenix had burned through All-Star point guards Jason Kidd and Stephon Marbury without achieving any lasting success. But the 2003–2004 season had been particularly challenging, with head coach Frank Johnson fired and replaced by assistant Mike D'Antoni after just six weeks, and stars Marbury and Penny Hardaway dispatched to New York in a blockbuster trade in January.

To top things off, the team had undergone an ownership change in late June that had seen an investment group led by Robert Sarver take control of the Suns. The trade of Marbury and the new ownership were two key factors in the Suns' hot pursuit of Steve Nash that July.

Now Steve faced the challenge of trying to lead the NBA's youngest team back into the playoff hunt in the hotly contested Western Conference. It was something he looked forward to, especially considering the presence of young stars Amare Stoudemire, Shawn Marion, Joe Johnson, and Leandro Barbosa, a quartet Steve believed had tremendous potential. The Suns had also signed free-agent shooting guard Quentin Richardson during the off-season, giving Steve another valuable weapon to work with in his new offense.

"I thought it would be a great fit," Steve says now of joining the Suns. "I was excited to try to take those guys and make them something better. That was an exciting part of it—not a detriment, as people may have thought, considering their win percentage the year before."

That optimism was well founded. When Steve Nash was added into the Phoenix mix—along with the aggressive game plan of Mike D'Antoni to constantly run the ball, freewheel on offense, and rely heavily on the three-pointer—the result was breathtaking.

Immediately, the Suns were a different team. Under Steve's leadership, they took the NBA by storm that season, finishing with a league-best 62 wins and only 20 losses. The victory total tied a Phoenix franchise record. The turnaround marked only the second time in NBA history that a team had recorded 60 wins immediately following a 50-loss season.

The Suns' starting five—Nash, Stoudemire, Richardson, Marion, and Johnson—was the most prolific in the league. As a team, Phoenix averaged 110.5 points per game, the highest scoring total in a decade. And the Suns smashed the single-season record for three-pointers with 796.

Benefiting greatly from the veteran leadership and toughness that they had sought when landing Steve, the young Suns finished 31–10 on the road during the season, the best showing in franchise history and the seventh-best of all time in the NBA. They also became one of the most popular draws in the league, with their run-and-gun style and their desire to put up a shot no more than seven seconds into each possession.

For the third time in his career, Steve was selected by coaches to play in the NBA All-Star Game. Joining him for the game in Denver were teammates Amare Stoudemire and Shawn Marion. Steve won the PlayStation Skills competition during All-Star Weekend, posting a record total of 25.4 seconds in the timed obstacle course that tests players' dribbling, passing, and shooting skills. Then he and Stoudemire teamed up to wow fans in the Pepsi Center and millions watching on television during the slam-dunk competition. Steve used his sterling soccer skills to set up Stoudemire's best dunk. On that attempt, the Phoenix power forward lobbed the ball off the glass. Steve then headed it back to Stoudemire who rammed it home one-handed. To top off the weekend, hulking Miami Heat center Shaquille O'Neal gave Steve an autographed pair of his size-22 sneakers, one for each of his twins, Lola and Bella.

The 2004–2005 campaign was a season in which everything seemed to go right for the Suns and for Steve Nash. With the multitude of weapons in the Phoenix lineup, he piled up by far the largest assist total of his career with 861, 174 more than he had dished out in his previous best NBA year. For the first time in his career, Steve led the NBA in assists with 11.5 per game, and he still managed to score at a 15.5-point per game clip while averaging a career-best 3.3 rebounds and shooting better than 50 percent from the field, an impressive percentage for a guard.

Perhaps more telling, however, were the career years his teammates enjoyed with Steve running the high-octane show. Amare Stoudemire and Joe Johnson both scored at a higher rate than ever before with Nash distributing the ball and running the Suns at breakneck speed. Injuries kept Steve out of the Suns lineup for seven games of the regular season, and during that time Phoenix looked like a completely different team, sputtering on offense, as they lost five of those contests.

The season began well for Steve, who won the NBA's Player of the Month honors for November by pacing the Suns to a league-best 12–2 record, and things just kept getting better from there. During the end of November and part of December the Suns won 11 straight games, and Steve eclipsed Magic Johnson's NBA record by recording at least 10 assists in each of those games.

On March 30, Steve posted the second triple-double of his career, scoring 12 points, pulling down 13 rebounds, and dishing off 12 assists against the Philadelphia 76ers. That performance came in just twenty-seven minutes of court time as the Suns rested Steve for the entire fourth quarter.

As the season progressed, speculation began to circulate that Steve might be among those considered for the NBA's Most Valuable Player award. But Shaquille O'Neal, who was posting big numbers after moving from the Los Angeles Lakers to the Miami Heat, was the heavy favorite for that prize.

On May 5, 2005, *The Arizona Republic* ran a story predicting that Steve would indeed be crowned the 2004–2005 NBA MVP. It based the story on its own unofficial poll, consulting 104 of the 127 writers and broadcasters who covered the league, the same people who officially voted on the award. The NBA was silent on the newspaper's story, preferring to wait until its own official announcement a few days later.

As speculation mounted, Steve was diplomatic, saying it was a thrill merely to be included in talk about the MVP award. "In a way, just to get this close, I feel like I've already won," he told reporters.

The Republic's story proved to be accurate. On Sunday, May 8, 2005, Steve was officially named league MVP during halftime of an NBA playoff telecast. After being informed about the win by the league the night before, Steve had chosen to celebrate by inviting the entire Suns training staff to his Phoenix home. After all, weren't these the folks who had been responsible for keeping him healthy and loose for an entire season?

Being named MVP wasn't really a dream come true for Steve, since he had never envisioned himself winning an award that typically goes to a prolific scorer or a much taller player. Nevertheless, it was a tremendous honor that left him feeling surprised and genuinely humbled.

"I definitely won this award because of my role on the team," Nash told reporters on the eve of the official announcement. "I didn't win this because I overpower people or I'm dominating people with physical ability, whether it's jumping ability or strength or height.

"I don't really know what to make of it. I didn't have any NBA players in my neighborhood. I don't even think I dreamed about this award. I don't know what to say. I just kept trying."

The Suns staged a press conference the next morning to formally announce the MVP selection, which by now was the NBA's worst-kept secret. For Steve, it all still seemed unreal. Thirteen years earlier, he had practically been forced to beg for a college scholarship. Now he was the most valuable player of the best basketball league on earth. He knew that in winning the MVP award he had become only the sixth guard in league history to do so, following legends Bob Cousy, Oscar Robertson, Magic Johnson, Michael Jordan, and Allen Iverson. He was just the third point guard after Cousy and Johnson to be named MVP. Steve was also only the second MVP in Phoenix franchise history—Charles Barkley was the other. And he was just the third foreign player to be honored with the award, following Hakeem Olajuwon of Nigeria and Tim Duncan of the Virgin Islands.

When asked how he felt about being linked forever to such a list of basketball greats, Steve paused for a second. Then he told reporters that it reminded him a bit of an old "Sesame Street" song, the one that starts "One of these things is not like the others …" which drew chuckles from the journalists in the room.

Seconds after he was handed the massive Maurice Podoloff Trophy by the Suns' Jerry Colangelo, Steve called the entire Phoenix team up on stage with him to share in the honor. The grinning players crowded around him, facing the cameras, clearly pleased for their point guard.

"It is uncomfortable to be singled out," Steve said in accepting the award. "To be in this position, in some ways, is difficult. This is a pinnacle of a player's career, individually, in many ways. But the pinnacle of a player's career is also defined by winning. So sixty-two wins is as big a pinnacle as winning the MVP. That's the only reason I'm in this position. It's very important to me to make sure my teammates know and the world knows this is due to my team's terrific character and camaraderie."

While many celebrated Steve's MVP win, some strongly disagreed with the choice, even going as far as to say his selection was influenced by race. It had been one of the closest MVP ballots in league history, with Steve receiving 65 first-place votes for a total of 1,066 points. Miami's Shaquille O'Neal finished with 58 first-place votes and 1,032 points.

Steve was the first white player since Larry Bird of the Boston Celtics in 1986 to win the MVP award. And since 1973, the only other white players to win the award had been Bird, who captured it three times; Portland big man Bill Walton; and Boston center Dave Cowens. There were some who believed that Steve was given more votes than he deserved by the sportswriters and broadcasters, many of whom are white themselves and perhaps subconsciously rooted for a small white point guard to capture the award.

Some pointed to the fact that Nash had averaged just 15.5 points per game as a prime reason why he should not have beaten out the dominant O'Neal for the award. The Heat center had posted impressive averages of 22.9 points and 10.4 rebounds in a terrific turnaround season for Miami.

Columnist Dan Le Batard of *The Miami Herald* was particularly provocative in his criticism of Nash's win.

"No one who looks or plays like Steve Nash has ever been basketball's MVP. Ever. In the history of the award, a tiny, one-dimensional point guard who plays no defense and averages fewer than 16 points a game never has won it," Le Batard wrote.

"But Nash just stole Shaquille O'Neal's trophy, even though O'Neal had much better numbers than Nash in just about every statistical measurement except assists, so it begs the question:

"Is this as black and white as the box scores that usually decide these things?"

For his part, O'Neal was gracious about Nash's MVP win. "He's a great guy," the Heat center told reporters. "It's been a good year for Steve. He had twins ... He is playing great basketball. Congratulations, Steve. Congratulations to the Canadian people. It's a great honor."

Suns coach Mike D'Antoni knew, perhaps better than anybody, the value of Nash to his team, and he staunchly defended the MVP selection. "It should be all about winning; it shouldn't be about anything else," the coach told reporters. "What I like about it is someone being an unselfish player and ... putting the team first and coming out on top. That's a pretty important message. You can score 15 points [per game] and be an MVP."

Steve's individual award was one of three picked up by the Suns during the 2004–2005 season. D'Antoni was named NBA Coach of the Year and team president Bryan Colangelo the Executive of the Year for a team that had managed the third-greatest turnaround in NBA history. Steve also cracked the All-NBA First Team for the first time in his career, while Amare Stoudemire, quickly emerging into the league's premier power forward and forming a terrifying tandem with Steve, made the Second Team. Shawn Marion was named to the Third Team.

Steve and the Suns weren't content with a terrific regular season and the lion's share of the league awards. They had designs on an NBA championship. Steve believed the Suns had the horses to accomplish that goal. And they opened the post-season strongly by sweeping the Memphis Grizzlies 4–0 in their first-round series.

That set up an interesting conference semifinal, particularly from Steve's perspective. Standing in the path of the Suns were the Dallas Mavericks, the team that had allowed the MVP to slip away to Phoenix as a free agent just months earlier.

It was during this series that Steve Nash would win over all but the most prejudiced of those who had been skeptical of his MVP credentials. Against the Mavericks—his former team, led by his best friend in the league, Dirk Nowitzki—Steve turned in the finest post-season performances of his career to date. The hard-fought series also captured the imagination of basketball fans everywhere as both teams employed a highly entertaining fast-break style.

With the Suns up 2–1 in the series and the Mavericks playing on home court, Steve turned in the biggest scoring output of any game in his career. Nash was everywhere, making 20 of 28 shots in the American Airlines Center to finish with 48 points. Still, the Mavericks prevailed to win the game 119–109 and even the series at 2–2.

After the Suns had lost, despite Nash's scoring heroics in Game 4, many believed Dallas had gained the upper hand in the series, especially considering the fact that Phoenix was without injured guard Joe Johnson, who had fractured his orbital bone on a hard fall to the floor in Game 2. But Steve came up big once again in Game 5, recording his first playoff triple-double, with 34 points, 12 assists, and 13 rebounds as the Suns regained control with a 114–108 victory.

Back at American Airlines Center in Dallas for the next game, Steve turned in another incredible performance as the Suns overcame a 16-point deficit to edge the Mavericks 130–126 in overtime and advance to the Western Conference finals for only the second time in franchise history.

In that decisive game, Steve hit a running three-pointer with less than six seconds left in regulation to force overtime, and then added another three-pointer in the extra period that gave Phoenix the lead for good. He finished the game with a Herculean 39 points, 12 assists, and 9 rebounds, just short of a second straight triple-double.

Jason Terry, the point guard who had replaced Nash in Dallas, enjoyed a terrific game, too, with 36 points. But he also failed to stop Steve from launching his final three-point attempt of regulation play. Nash had stunned the Mavericks' fans by scoring 8 points in the final minute of regulation and adding 7 more in overtime. During the biggest moments of his career, he sank his last five shots in a row.

The victory sent Phoenix, a team that had failed to make the playoffs the previous season, into the Western Conference finals against the San Antonio Spurs. And while the Spurs would prove too much for the upstart Suns to handle, Steve would nevertheless shine in the showcase.

In Game 1 at Phoenix, he scored 29 points and added 13 assists in a 121–114 loss. The next game, he had 29 points and 15 assists as the Suns fell 111–108. Steve very nearly tied up that game with a running three-point attempt at the buzzer that bounced off the rim.

Those two performances made Steve the first player in NBA playoff history to record four straight games of at least 25 points and 10 assists. In doing so, he moved ahead of Oscar Robertson and Michael Jordan, two of the greatest names in the pro game.

Even the return of Joe Johnson to the Phoenix lineup for Game 3 couldn't turn things around for the Suns, however. The Spurs took complete control of the series with a 102–92 win at home in Game 3, holding Phoenix to just 39 first-half points and limiting Steve to just 1 assist through the first three quarters and 3 in total for the game. In his worst outing of the series, Steve had 20 points but also 6 turnovers.

The Spurs had hoped to wrap up the series in Game 4 at San Antonio, but they were beaten 111–106 by the resilient Suns, who weren't ready to end their season just yet. Steve bounced back with 17 points and 12 assists, but it was Amare Stoudemire who made the difference in this one, scoring 31 points and blocking Tim Duncan spectacularly on a late-game dunk attempt.

Heading back to Phoenix for Game 5, the Suns tried desperately to extend the series. But Duncan took control, scoring 31 points and adding 15 rebounds as San Antonio wrapped up the series with a 101–95 win. The victory gave the Spurs an NBA Finals berth for the second time in three years and the third time in seven seasons.

Steve Nash had 21 points and 10 assists in the game as his finest NBA season came to a distinctly unsatisfactory end.

Still, the playoffs had been a wonderful showcase for the league's unlikely MVP. Steve had averaged 23.9 points, 11.3 assists, and 4.8 rebounds while shooting better than 50 percent from the field and playing over forty minutes per game. Most of those who had doubted his value as MVP were won over by his heroic post-season effort.

"In some ways, we got almost all we could ask for out of this season, except the one thing we really wanted," Steve told reporters after the loss. "In many ways, it diminishes everything we accomplished this year, but hopefully in time we will be able to look back and really feel proud of our accomplishments and really enjoy them more than right now.

"You've got to take your lumps somewhere along the line, to be a champion. And hopefully this is one of those building blocks to be something better."

Steve Nash would wrap up 2005 on a much higher note. In June, just weeks after the end of the playoffs, he and Alejandra were married. In December, Steve was named winner of the Lou Marsh Trophy as Canada's outstanding athlete that year. Days later, he also received the Canadian Press Male Athlete of the Year Award for 2005.

14

THE SUN RISES...
AGAIN

"I would never have dreamed of being MVP first of all, let alone twice."

—Steve Nash, two-time NBA MVP, 2006

Despite the resounding success of the Phoenix Suns in 2004–2005, Steve Nash returned for his second season in the desert to a team barely recognizable as the lineup that he had steered to sixty-two regular-season wins the previous year.

Over the summer, the Suns had declined to match a generous US$70-million Atlanta Hawks offer to shooting guard Joe Johnson, an integral member of the 2004–2005 Phoenix team. As a result, Johnson was ultimately sent to the Hawks in a sign-and-trade deal. Coming the Suns' way was guard-forward Boris Diaw, then a little-known two-year NBA veteran originally from France.

Off-guard Quentin Richardson, another of the Suns' top offensive threats from the previous season, had also been traded—dealt to the New York Knicks in exchange for veteran center Kurt Thomas. The Phoenix brain trust believed Thomas would help solidify the Suns' inside and free up Amare Stoudemire to roam the paint as a power forward. But the major problem with that plan was that Amare Stoudemire was no longer available to the Suns. He had undergone complicated microfracture knee surgery over the summer and now wasn't expected to play until at least February.

So as Steve approached the second season of his second stint in Phoenix, only athletic do-everything forward Shawn Marion remained from the starters who had dominated the NBA alongside him the previous winter. Besides Diaw, newcomers to the team included defensive guard Raja Bell, small forward James Jones, sharpshooting guard Eddie House, and veteran power forward Brian Grant. Instead of returning to an established juggernaut, Steve now faced yet another rebuilding process. When these Suns opened up training camp in October 2005 at Tucson, they practically needed nametags.

With the departure of two starters and the absence of Stoudemire for at least the first half of the season, many NBA observers felt the Suns would struggle simply to make the playoffs in the competitive Western Conference, let alone repeat their glory year of 2004–2005. And with the sudden lack of firepower in the Phoenix lineup, few gave Steve Nash much of a chance to repeat as the league MVP, either.

After the Suns lost out in their free-agent pursuit of Steve's former Dallas teammate Michael Finley in August, many seemed ready to write off Phoenix's season before it had even begun. But Suns coach Mike D'Antoni disagreed.

"We still have two All-Stars, including the MVP of the league, so I'm not buying all the doomsday stuff," D'Antoni told reporters as the season began. "When you have a Steve Nash controlling the ball, it makes a big difference. At home or on the road, in the first quarter or the fourth quarter, he's going to get you where you need to go and the shots it takes to get there. So I expect we'll be a good team."

The Suns' doubters gained some momentum, however, after Phoenix stumbled slightly to begin the regular season, limping out to a 4–5 record. But once the new-look Suns lineup found its legs, it would turn in another superb season in the desert, one that proved the skeptics wrong and surprised even the team's staunchest supporters.

The Suns would have to go nearly the entire season without the powerful Stoudemire, who aborted a March comeback attempt after just three games and had to undergo minor surgery on his other knee. They also lost Kurt Thomas, who was supposed to provide extra depth inside to Stoudemire, after Thomas suffered a stress fracture to his right foot in late February. Somehow, though, despite the injuries and the changes, the Suns soldiered on in 2005–2006, with Steve again playing the ringmaster's role and drawing the most out of every player on his team.

Versatile forward Shawn Marion, new free-agent shooting guard acquisition Raja Bell, and the vastly underrated Boris Diaw all enjoyed career years with Steve at the helm. Diaw's transformation, in particular, was striking as he went from an unimposing bench player scoring 4.8 points per game in Atlanta to a key factor for the Suns, tallying 13.3 points per contest and often dominating with his passing skills and feel for the game. Marion posted career-best averages of 21.8 points and 11.8 rebounds as well as 60 double-doubles during an impressive season in which he also was touted as a possible candidate for league MVP. And Bell managed career-bests of 14.7 points and 3.2 rebounds per game and provided the Suns with tough perimeter defense. Three other Suns—James Jones, Leandro Barbosa, and Eddie House—also enjoyed career years.

Meanwhile, Steve Nash managed to do something that nobody predicted he would do, particularly without Stoudemire in the lineup. The thirty-two-year-old point guard improved his own statistics significantly, turning in a career year to follow up his MVP campaign of 2004–2005. Steve shot a career-best .512 from the field—outstanding for a guard—to average 18.8 points per game in 2005–2006, more than 3 points per night better than the previous season. He also shot 92 percent from the free-throw line, his best mark as a pro, to lead the league in that category. Steve's assists declined slightly, from 11.5 to 10.5 per game, but he was nevertheless the NBA's top playmaker for the second straight year. In all, he managed career highs in six categories and made the All-NBA First Team for the second consecutive year.

Perhaps most impressive, however, was the fact that Steve Nash pushed Phoenix close to replicating its 62-win season, despite the loss of Stoudemire and the departure of Richardson and Johnson. The Suns finished with a 54–28 record to win the Pacific Division for the second straight year. They resumed their role as the league's poster boys for how the game of basketball should be played, with speed and style. Once again, they free-wheeled for an entire season to lead the NBA in points scored, more than 108 per game.

Besides his statistical improvement, Steve also broke new ground for himself in the NBA when, for the first time, he was voted by fans to be a starter for the 2006 All-Star Game in Houston. Steve's newfound popularity was reflected in the fact that he trailed only Kobe Bryant among Western Conference guards in the fan balloting, gathering more than 1.8 million votes.

Meanwhile, despite celebrating his thirty-second birthday in February, Steve was physically feeling great, thanks in large part to a regime of corrective exercises and manual therapy from Aaron Nelson, the Suns' head athletic trainer. It was also Nelson who initiated Steve's practice of lying flat on his back on the sidelines when-ever he is resting during a game, rather than sitting in a seat, in order to keep his chronic back condition from flaring up.

"I feel younger almost every year," he told *The Arizona Republic* as his tenth NBA season progressed. "I feel like

I'm getting better every year. I feel like the season gets easier for me the last two years. It's nice to feel good at thirty-two. I don't feel old. I don't feel like this is getting harder. I feel like this is getting easier, if anything."

By February, Steve's name was also surfacing again as a possible repeat candidate for the NBA's Most Valuable Player award. "He's got my vote so far. What he is doing without Amare, and with so many new faces, is just incredible and a testament to the player he is," TNT analyst and former NBA head coach Doug Collins told the *East Valley Tribune.*

"All those critics of Steve Nash last year, they should all shut up," added former Suns great Charles Barkley. "What he's done so far, what he's accomplished, takes the steam out of every argument."

By April, General Mills, the makers of perhaps the most famous cereal in the United States, concurred with Barkley's assessment when they announced that they were putting Steve Nash on his own Wheaties box. The bright-orange box would feature Steve in a purple Suns uniform driving the basketball up the floor. Steve considered it a great honor to join the list of basketball legends—including Michael Jordan, Larry Bird, Jerry West, and Bob Cousy—who have had their likeness on the cereal known as the "Breakfast of Champions." He himself had never eaten the cereal as a kid because Wheaties isn't sold in Canada. But now Steve realized that thousands of children would be looking at his picture every morning as they poured their breakfast into a bowl.

While they were wrapping up awards and accolades, Steve and the Suns also benefited in the spring of 2006 from a quirk in the NBA's playoff system—one that has since been corrected. Despite having only the third-best record in the Western Conference, the Suns were able to avoid meeting either the Dallas Mavericks or the San Antonio Spurs—teams that had finished ahead of them—in the first two rounds of the playoffs.

The Suns instead drew the Los Angeles Lakers and their star guard Kobe Bryant, a rival of Steve's for the MVP award who had scored 81 points in a single regular-season game against the Toronto Raptors. Before the opening-round series began, the media hyped this as a delicious matchup of MVP heavyweights and the dramatic series certainly didn't disappoint.

Steve wasted little time setting the tone for the series as he scored 20 points, added 10 assists, and hit a three-pointer with 1:07 remaining that powered the Suns to a 107–102 win over Los Angeles in the series opener. But after that victory, Bryant and the Lakers proceeded to put the Suns on the ropes, winning the next three straight to take a commanding 3–1 series lead.

The Lakers' third victory was particularly demoralizing for the Suns and their MVP point guard. In that epic game, Los Angeles edged the Suns 99–98 in overtime as Bryant turned in one of the most memorable performances of a brilliant career, hitting two clutch shots to first tie and then win the game.

Both dramatic plays came at the expense of Steve Nash, who uncharacteristically coughed up the ball at two key junctures. With the Suns leading 90–88 and in possession of the ball in the dying seconds of regulation play, Steve lost his footing and was stripped by Los Angeles guard Smush Parker near midcourt. Devean George recovered the ball and found Bryant, who dribbled downcourt and hit a floating runner with seven-tenths of a second left, to force overtime.

With fifty seconds left in the overtime session, Steve hit a three to give Phoenix a 98–95 lead. After Bryant scored to bring the Lakers to within a point, Steve once again had the ball in his hands and the Suns seemed to be in control. With 6.1 seconds left, however, Nash was tied up by the Lakers' Luke Walton as teammate Boris Diaw attempted in vain to call a time-out. The result was a jump-ball at center court, which the much larger Walton won. Bryant pursued the loose ball, dribbled to the right side of the key, and calmly nailed a seventeen-footer to give the Lakers the shocking victory and a seemingly insurmountable 3–1 lead in the series.

The loss put Steve Nash and the Suns in a serious hole. Only seven teams in NBA history had ever overcome a 3–1 series deficit. Steve realized this better than anyone, and he blamed himself for the mistakes. He had scored 22 points and dished out 11 assists in the hard-fought game, but the two crucial errors bothered him. So did the fact that he had shot just 2-for-11 in the second half.

Steve would call that game "as tough a loss as you could face." But he gave Bryant credit for coming through in the clutch. "It was amazing," he told reporters. "He had two opportunities and made two great shots."

Privately, Steve fumed at the turnovers he had committed. Although he felt he had been fouled on the tie-up by Walton in overtime, he told former high school coach Ian Hyde-Lay, in an e-mail not long after the game, that he had been completely at fault for the loss.

"Boy, the great thing about sport is you don't have to wait too long before you get another chance to get back and redeem yourself," Steve wrote his former coach.

As it turned out, he was right. In Game 5, the Suns beat the Lakers 114–97, scoring 13 straight points in the fourth quarter to take control. Steve had 22 points and was one of six Suns in double figures as Phoenix staved off elimination.

Game 6 would be the key to the series for both teams. The Lakers wanted to finish things off in front of actor Jack Nicholson and the rest of the star-studded front-row fan base at the Staples Center in Los Angeles. The Suns needed another win just to stay alive.

Phoenix was facing an uphill battle without guard and key defensive stopper Raja Bell, who was serving a one-game suspension for hitting Kobe Bryant in the throat with his arm in Game 5. But despite the absence of Bell and a 50-point night from Bryant, the Suns managed to beat the Lakers 126–118 in overtime on the strength of a miraculous shot by forward Tim Thomas.

Thomas had been claimed on waivers by Phoenix late in the regular season and had evolved into a key playoff performer. In this game, he took a pass from Steve with 6.3 seconds left in the fourth quarter and calmly nailed a long three to send the game into overtime. Steve led the way for the Suns, more than atoning for his Game 4 miscues by contributing 32 points and 13 assists to set up a Game 7 back in Phoenix.

As it turned out, Game 6 had produced all the drama, however. In the deciding game at Phoenix, the Lakers were simply no match for the home-court Suns, falling 121–90. Phoenix had survived, in the process becoming the first NBA team in thirty-six years to lose three straight games in a playoff series and still prevail.

The victory sent Steve and the Suns into the second round of the 2006 playoffs against the Los Angeles Clippers, a much bigger and potentially more dangerous opponent. Once again, the Suns opened on the right note as Nash had 31 points and 12 assists in a 130–123 Phoenix win. But over the next five games, three of which were won by the Clippers, fatigue and a sore back began to wear Steve down. The Clippers' constant double-teams on the Suns star seemed to be paying dividends, and other Phoenix players weren't stepping up enough to shoulder the offensive load.

The Suns were in fact fortunate not to be trailing the series 3–2 heading back to Los Angeles. They needed a miracle three-pointer from Raja Bell with 1.1 seconds left in the first overtime period to stay alive. They finally prevailed 125–118 in the second extra session to instead send the Clippers home down a game.

But the Clippers bounced back to win Game 6, 118–106, putting the Suns into their second Game 7 showdown in as many series. The bonus for Phoenix was that a quirk in the NBA schedule allowed for three days' rest before the sudden-death game. The time off did wonders for Steve, who came through with 29 points and 11 assists in a 127–107 victory. Prior to that contest, his tired legs had contributed to Steve shooting just 2-for-18 from three-point range over the previous five games of the series. In the heat of Game 7, Steve went 11-for-16 from the field.

The win over the Clippers sent Steve and the Suns into a playoff showdown against his old team, the Dallas Mavericks, for the second straight spring. But this time the stakes were higher, because this meeting came in the Western Conference finals. As Steve prepared to face his good friend and former teammate Dirk Nowitzki, he knew that at least one of them would be realizing a dream by playing in the NBA finals that spring. Despite their longtime friendship, he wanted to be that one.

Once again, the Suns jumped out to a quick series lead, beating Dallas 121–118 in the opener at the American Airlines Center. And once again, Steve turned in a huge game when the stakes were high, scoring 27 points, including 10 in the final 3:28.

However, the series-opening victory didn't come without cost to the Suns, who lost valuable guard Raja Bell to a strained left calf that would severely hamper him for the rest of the series and ultimately harm Phoenix's chances of advancing.

With Bell added to the already considerable list of Phoenix wounded, the depleted Suns dropped the next two games to trail Dallas 2–1 in the series. That included a 95–88 defeat in Game 3 at Phoenix, after which Steve took his teammates to task publicly for their approach to the series.

"We're out there with our shoulders slumped and we're not smiling. We're not fighting. We're not, you know, playing with the necessary fire it takes to win," he told reporters. "I think that the most disappointing thing is just the way we're going out there and playing."

The pep talked seemed to work, as the Suns rebounded to rout the Mavericks 106–86 in Game 4, evening the series. Steve scored 21 points and helped key a 29–6 run in the third and fourth quarters that decided the game.

But the series, and the entire playoffs for the Suns, would hinge on the fifth game in Dallas. In that contest, Phoenix seemingly had the home-court Mavericks on the ropes, down by 7 points in the third quarter. That's when Dallas forward Dirk Nowitzki came alive, erupting for a 50-point night as the Mavericks roared back to win 117–101 and take a 3–2 lead despite a 20-point, 11-assist effort by Steve.

The next defeat was much more difficult for Steve and the Suns to stomach, however. They led by as many as 18 points in the second quarter before completely running out of gas and allowing the visiting Mavericks to win the game 102–93 and take the series by a 4–2 margin.

It marked the first trip to the NBA finals in Mavericks franchise history, and the second Western Conference finals loss in as many springs for the Suns.

"I don't know if you can pin it all on fatigue, but I also think it would be ignorant not to say it played a part," a disappointed Steve said after the playoffs had ended for his shorthanded team.

Mavericks owner Mark Cuban seemed to be trying to rub a little salt in Steve's wounds when he appeared on *The Late Show with David Letterman* in the middle of the NBA finals, which his Dallas club would eventually lose to the Miami Heat. When asked by Letterman, essentially, if letting Steve go to Phoenix had been a mistake, Cuban replied, "Steve's a great guy. I love him to death. But why couldn't he play like an MVP for us? All's well that ends well…. Jason Terry took his place, and look where we are. And he's home watching."

Steve says now that Cuban's words didn't bother him. "I would expect that from him," he said. "It wasn't really like anything shocking when somebody told me [what Cuban had said]. You know, he is what he is. He loves to hear himself talk, really. And whatever, it's no big deal."

Months later, though, Steve could admit that losing to Dallas hurt a little more than if the defeat had come against another club.

"You know it was difficult that they were going to the finals," he says now. "But at the same time, I felt like we had all the injuries, and they were a better team than us with their depth. They deserved it. They played better."

In the midst of the first-round series against the Lakers, *The Arizona Republic* ran a story, citing a league source, saying that Steve would win the MVP award for a second straight year. If true, this would mark only the ninth time in league history that a player had repeated as Maurice

Podoloff Trophy winner, and it would vault Steve into a hallowed group that includes Michael Jordan, Magic Johnson, Larry Bird, and Wilt Chamberlain. Johnson, one of Steve's idols as he grew up in Victoria, was the only other point guard to have won it twice in a row.

"Any time you sit back and think about just winning it once, it's mind-boggling—the company and what it means in the history of the game," Steve told reporters after *The Republic* story broke. "To win it twice obviously just compounds that. It's an incredible honor. It's a tribute to what this game allows people to do if they work hard."

The rumor was true, and the award was officially announced during a May 7 press conference in Phoenix. This time around, the voting wasn't even close. Steve recorded 57 first-place votes from the panel of 125 writers and broadcasters who cover the NBA, to finish with 924 total points. Cleveland's young phenom LeBron James was next with 16 first-place votes and 688 points. Steve's good friend Dirk Nowitzki of the Dallas Mavericks—the player with whom he had endured those early dog days in Dallas—ended up third, with 14 first-place votes and 544 points.

"I have to admit, it's a little bit uncomfortable to be singled out amongst all these great players two years in a row," Steve said upon accepting the award. "I have to pinch myself. I couldn't believe it last year, and to do it again is even more difficult to understand.

"But I'm not gonna give it back."

Once again, voters had singled out Steve for making his teammates better. Six other Suns besides him had posted career highs in scoring during 2005–2006, and Boris Diaw had become the NBA's Most Improved Player after joining Nash and the Suns. But Steve told those at the press conference that the benefits extended both ways. "A lot is made about me making my teammates better, and I really believe that my teammates make me a lot better, too."

Although Steve and the Suns have fallen short of their ultimate goal in the playoffs during his two seasons back in Arizona, he realizes he has already accomplished more than most thought was possible when he left Dallas in 2004.

"I would never have dreamed of being MVP first of all, let alone twice," Steve says now. "And I don't think I necessarily knew we'd be in the conference finals two years in a row and win as many games as we have. You know, I definitely thought we could compete and we'd be up there, but to actually have done it and got to the [league] semifinals twice in a row is probably more than anybody bargained for when I signed there."

Another unexpected accolade came to Steve in September 2006. He was invited to speak at Santa Clara University's commencement exercises and while he was there he attended a ceremony in which the Broncos retired his jersey. Steve's number 11 now hangs in the rafters of the Leavey Center, making him the first Santa Clara athlete to be honored in this way. Steve described the experience as "amazing and very humbling."

The ultimate prize, of course, is an NBA championship. It was one of the goals Steve set for himself when he entered the league as a rookie back in 1996. And it is the one major achievement that has eluded him during his sterling career to date.

The ten-year NBA veteran believes the Suns have the potential to realize that goal over the next couple of years, particularly if Amare Stoudemire can return to his previous rim-rattling form and Phoenix can avoid the run of injuries that plagued it in 2005–2006.

"I think we can do it," Steve says. "I think a lot of it depends on our health. Last year, obviously we were struggling for our fitness with a lot of guys—Amare being the obvious one. But you know in the semifinals we had a chance to beat Dallas if Raja was healthy. He was banged up, we were already really thin and didn't have a lot of options, so when he was playing on one leg ...

"But you know, we were winning every game of that series at halftime and just not to have the depth to close four of them out.... You wonder what this team would have been like even if we just had him healthy, let alone having Amare or whoever else was [injured]."

Considering Steve's track record against seemingly insurmountable odds, it won't be surprising if he reaches his ultimate goal of a NBA championship ring sometime soon. But he would be the first to tell you that no one player does this alone and, in the end, it will be a combination of teamwork, tenacity, and good fortune that takes him to that title.

15

ONE OF A KIND

It is halftime at the 2006 Steve Nash Foundation Charity Classic basketball game in Vancouver. But the star of the evening isn't in the locker room catching a breather, or even on the sidelines watching the entertainment with his family and teammates. No, Steve Nash *is* the entertainment.

Out on the glistening hardwood floor of General Motors Place, Steve is putting on a clinic. A soccer clinic. He and popular freestyle soccer skills entertainer Steve Elias are heading the ball between each other, back and forth, to and fro, with spellbinding control.

The soccer ball bounces off the shoulders, feet, and heads of the two Steves countless times, volleying between them without touching the floor. Gradually, while still keeping it aloft, they move downcourt, attempting the grand finale several times before Nash finally heads the ball triumphantly through the basket.

The crowd of more than sixteen thousand goes wild. Nash is clearly loving it too. At the end of the exhibition he wraps Elias in a huge hug. He has enjoyed himself as much as any of the thousands of wide-eyed kids who just took in the latest unexpected, dazzling display from their hero.

Not exactly your average NBA superstar.

There is not much that is average about Steve Nash, athletically or otherwise, despite what he might argue. He grew up as an outstanding young athlete in Canada but didn't gravitate to hockey. He played the game, and was good enough to be identified early on as a potential junior prospect, but hockey wasn't his first love. That was soccer, which his father had played semi-professionally, first in his native England and later in South Africa.

Steve cheered for the Spurs as a youngster, but not, like many of his NBA teammates, the San Antonio Spurs. Instead, the Tottenham Hotspurs of English soccer was—and still is—the side he supports with a passion. His first word as a baby, tellingly, was "GOAALLL!" delivered in the excited, over-the-top stylings of South American soccer announcers. Despite Steve's considerable accomplishments, until recently younger brother Martin was the more famous Nash with their family in England, because he has played soccer in that country's first division and appeared in thirty games for Canada internationally. And sister Joann also excelled at "the beautiful game," serving as captain of the University of Victoria Vikes women's squad for three seasons.

Steve was a standout basketball player in high school, as the vast majority of his NBA counterparts were. But few of them played just one season of high school ball, or hailed from the hoops hinterland of Canada, or had to sweat it out to see whether they'd get even a single college scholarship offer.

"I always felt like I could get there," Steve says now of his unusual path to the peak of the basketball world. "I always felt like I could improve, and I think there were many times that built on top of each other—where you realized you can do it, you can keep improving. You can't really pick one as the turning point, but there are a lot of moments that add to your belief and confidence."

Steve's high school coach from Victoria knows there is something different inside Steve, something extra that has allowed him to travel a path so unlikely that even Hollywood would reject the script as implausible.

"I think there are lots of athletes who, if there are five pieces that you need, might have four of them, but they don't have five. They always just fall short because one of those things is missing. Well, nothing's missing there for Steve. He's got everything," says Ian Hyde-Lay. "He's got amazing skill. He has amazing work ethic. He has very, very strong core values and principles. He's an incredible leader. I mean, he's a great athlete."

It is interesting that Hyde-Lay uses the word "athlete" because, in NBA circles, Steve Nash is frequently described as "non-athletic." Never mind that Steve excelled in every sport he attempted while growing up on Vancouver Island. He was a B.C. high school champion in soccer, basketball, and rugby and won provincial tournament MVP honors in two of those three sports. He was considered a legitimate hockey and baseball prospect, and was talented with a lacrosse stick, as well. In Grade 10, a skinny Steve even won the provincial discus competition.

The reason he is not recognized as "athletic" is that he doesn't match the stereotypical version of that adjective, at least not in the NBA. He doesn't jump out of the gym like many pro basketball stars. But there is so much more to being an athlete than possessing one or two world-class physical skills. And contrary to popular belief, Steve can dunk a basketball.

"The thing that people don't know about Steve is that, although he isn't a leaper, he has the most amazing body control I have ever seen in an athlete," says Dallas Mavericks owner Mark Cuban, his former NBA boss. "He can contort his body to get off a shot from any angle, going up, or coming down. The shots he has made have made circus acts look boring."

Al Whitley has a unique perspective on Steve Nash's athletic ability. He ran alongside Steve as a seven-year-old minor soccer player in Victoria in the early 1980s. He played more one-on-one basketball in his driveway against Steve than he can possibly recall. And he traveled North America with Steve, watching his lifelong buddy play for the Dallas Mavericks during three standout NBA seasons.

"You know, it was easy to tell Steve was a phenomenal athlete when we were kids," Whitley says. "He excelled and was terrific at every sport he played. But to the extent of where he's taken those abilities and having reached the level he's obviously playing at now, I don't think anyone could have seen that at an early age."

Whitley believes that it is what is inside Nash's heart, his spirit, that makes him a tremendous athlete, more than any physical trait.

"Steve's one of the most competitive people I know. And any time he's ever been doubted or second-guessed in his life, he's always seemed to prove those people wrong. He just has some type of inner strength about him that, really, I haven't seen in too many guys, where nothing short of success is acceptable," Whitley says.

"To do what he's doing and to continue to get better every year as he gets older is very, very rare in professional sports, and especially in the NBA. You know, a lot of people would say that, at thirty-two, he'd be on the down-side of his career. But really if you look at what he's done the last couple of years, he only seems to be getting better."

Mark Cuban, whose team made the NBA finals in 2006, two years after letting Steve slip away to free agency, says he hasn't been surprised at what Nash has accomplished in Phoenix.

"Nothing about Steve surprises me," Cuban says. "I think the Suns' coaching staff used Steve's talents better than we had, and Steve thrived on that. It's a tribute to Steve, his ability to communicate, his ability as a player, and to the Suns."

Cuban says the fact that the Mavericks beat the Suns in the 2006 Western Conference finals proves nothing one way or another about whether allowing Steve to leave Dallas was the right move.

"There are so many dynamics that go into making a basketball team successful," the Mavericks' owner says.

"So much of it is style of play, luck, and timing. Steve has been successful his entire career and made every team he has been on better. We made a coaching change the year Steve left. Had the change been made a year earlier, Steve may have been an MVP for the Mavs. You never know!"

The telephone rings. It is Steve Nash calling from Manhattan, where he spends his summers living in a two-story apartment in Tribeca with his wife Alejandra and their twin toddlers, Lola and Bella.

Judging by the honks and assorted street noise in the background, you sense that he is in traffic somewhere, calling from a cell phone. You are correct. Except he's not driving his sleek Mercedes AMG convertible. He is on much smaller wheels. A skateboard.

Steve Nash's summer routine is pretty much set. Three mornings a week, he leaves his apartment with his skateboard in tow, taking the subway to a gym where he works out with his personal trainer. He then skateboards to a second Manhattan gym, where he practices basketball and, you guessed it, soccer. Then it's back on the skateboard, rolling down the popular West Side Highway bicycle and inline-skating path that runs along the Hudson River, all the way home.

Not exactly your average NBA superstar's mode of travel.

Quirky. How else would you describe Steve Nash when set against the backdrop of professional basketball? How many NBA players get around by skateboard and subway? How many get their kicks out of three soccer games a week in Manhattan summer leagues?

Steve defies NBA stereotypes. He is small, at least by basketball standards, he is Canadian, and he is quietly modest. So quiet that reporters often have to strain their ears and jack up the sensitivity of their microphones to catch what he's saying.

His game is different, too. It's high-paced, frenetic, water-bug-style basketball, and it's extremely unselfish. In a league where paychecks inflate in direct ratio to points scored, he still prefers to pass.

And then there's the hair. Until he shaved off his unruly locks in July 2006 and showed up at his charity basketball game in Vancouver almost unrecognizable, Steve possessed easily the most famous mane in basketball. Virtually every description of Nash, in every feature story or television script since the 2000 Olympics, referred to him as "shaggy-haired" or "mop-topped" or "hairstyle-challenged." One sportswriter once described his former do as an "egg-beater" special. It even made ESPN.com's honor roll for the "worst sports hair of 2003." Joining Steve on that list were National Football League coach Jimmy Johnson, Brazilian soccer star Ronaldo, and former NBA bad-boy Dennis Rodman. Of Steve's hair, the comment was simply: "When ball boys are unavailable, doubles as sweat mop."

It is February 2003 and Steve Nash is sitting in a hotel ballroom in Atlanta, Georgia. He is appearing at a "media availability session," part of his obligation at the NBA's All-Star Weekend.

Nash, as usual, has a different look about him than the rest of the players. He is casual, sporting an olive-green T-shirt that bears an image of a person shooting a basketball. The caption reads: "No War. Shoot for Peace." Steve is wearing the T-shirt in front of hundreds of American reporters at roughly the same time the United States is preparing to embark on a controversial war in Iraq. His choice of wardrobe is not a coincidence.

The shirt has come from an old high school friend, who is an activist at the University of British Columbia. "These are just people who really want to make change and help the world and, looking at myself introspectively, I don't do enough on my part to help people," he tells the All-Star media throng.

Steve knows he is taking a risk. At the time, he plays for a team in Dallas, home state to President George W. Bush and a place that tends to tilt toward the conservative side of the ledger when it comes to such matters.

"I'm not telling anyone to believe in what I believe in. I just want people to educate themselves as I'm trying to," Steve explains to the media. "This is just a statement for us all to get involved and to learn more about things so that we can make a more informed decision. I just think people need to be pro-active right now, because we're in a dangerous time in history."

Not exactly your typical NBA superstar sound bites.

Steve Nash is obviously not your average NBA interview. He would rather discuss just about anything than himself. When the talk turns to a childhood friend, his family, soccer, music, or a good book, he becomes much more animated than when he is trying to describe why he has overcome great odds and been so successful in the NBA.

Of course, he is more than willing to offer his analysis of games and players and basketball trends, insight that has made him a popular member of the NBA's annual All-Interview Team, chosen by journalists who cover the league.

Steve has come a long way from the Grade 11 kid at Mount Douglas Secondary who didn't care much for studying. He has a degree in Sociology from Santa Clara University, but he has become more of a scholar since leaving that school. He is a voracious reader, especially when his team is on the road and he has time to sample the pages of everything from John Steinbeck to Fyodor Dostoevsky, John Feinstein to Ernest Hemingway.

Obviously, he has beliefs about world affairs, too. And during the Atlanta All-Star Game he decided to use his fame as a platform to encourage others to educate themselves on global events. He took some heat for his outspokenness, with a few fans calling him a "Communist" and telling him to go back to Canada.

"The one thing that Steve represents that makes him special is that he pays attention to what is happening around the world," says Mark Cuban. "Many who are successful in a business or sport get a case of tunnel vision and don't look at the world around them. Steve is the exact opposite. That's what I miss most about him not being on the Mavs—not his ability on the court, but his awareness and willingness to discuss all that is life off the court.

"Steve uses basketball to experience and understand life—basketball doesn't use him. That's an important message that everyone should hopefully understand about him and apply to their own jobs and lives."

It is that awareness, in part, that prompted *Time Magazine* in May 2006 to name Steve Nash one of its "100 People Who Shape Our World." Steve was listed among the "heroes and pioneers" section, which also included the likes of Al Gore, Ralph Lauren, Paul Simon, Bill Clinton, Bono, and Angelina Jolie. The magazine asked former Suns superstar Charles Barkley to write its entry on Steve for the feature spread.

"I've been all over the world, and I always think people won't know who I am. They do," Barkley wrote. "The way basketball has been embraced globally always amazes me. And I'm glad the world has got a chance to learn from a guy like Steve Nash.

"What has he taught us? It pays to be selfless…. Over the past few years, his popularity has exploded. His ego could have swelled—everyone else's does. But he still just wants to pass the ball.

"I'm a lucky guy to be living in Phoenix. The sun. The golf. And I get to watch Nash act like a magician on the court. Can't top that. And who knows? Maybe he'll inspire a whole new generation of kids to pass out of double-teams the way he does. Like Nash, maybe they'll be selfless off the court, too. That would be even better."

It is May 1996, and a twenty-two-year-old Steve Nash is counting the days until he will be drafted into the National Basketball Association, realizing a lifelong dream. In the meantime, he is sitting in his family's Victoria home, speaking for the umpteenth time to a local reporter who has decided to write a book on him.

The reporter has brought along his three-year-old daughter for the interview session. Naturally, she grows restless waiting through all the talk about Steve's high school career, his days at Santa Clara, the upcoming draft, and what he thinks about joining the NBA. The tiny blond toddler begins to fuss.

The reporter looks up from the notebook in which he has been scribbling. As Steve Nash has been patiently answering the questions, he has also simultaneously hauled out a large plastic tub full of his kid sister's dolls. He is now playing Barbies with the little girl, helping her to cut through the tedium of accompanying Dad to work.

Not exactly your average NBA MVP.

Steve Nash is all about assists—on the court and off. It's that simple. Somewhere on his way to becoming an NBA millionaire, he decided that he had a responsibility to share his good fortune.

That spirit most likely originates from his parents, John and Jean, who established a warm, supportive household and taught their children to think of others besides themselves.

In 2001, Steve established the Steve Nash Foundation, a charity dedicated to "assisting underserved children in their health, personal development, education, and enjoyment of life." The foundation raised nearly $650,000 through charity basketball games in 2005 and 2006 in Toronto and Vancouver, respectively. It funds the Steve Nash Youth Basketball League in British Columbia, which now includes more than 8,000 players province-wide. It has also contributed heavily to the future construction of an all-kids, all-access basketball facility in Greater Toronto.

Perhaps the most impressive project for the foundation thus far, however, has been the outfitting of a new post-operative pediatric cardiology ward at Hospital de Clinicas in Asunción, Paraguay. Through donations from Steve and Alejandra, as well as other private supporters and corporations, the foundation has been able to provide a place for vulnerable babies to receive the critical care they need at the facility known as Paraguay's "Hospital of the Poor."

At Steve's charity game in July 2006, ten courtside seats were reserved for kids from the Strathcona Community Centre, located on Vancouver's beleaguered Downtown Eastside. More importantly, the Steve Nash Foundation has also committed to help garner support to build a new kitchen at the centre, which feeds more than 250 children breakfast each morning. Steve's kid sister, Joann, the foundation's program director, helps dish out those early meals every Wednesday.

Steve says he was like other youngsters growing up in the comfort of middle-class Canada. He was "oblivious, for the most part" to the fact other kids around the world were poor and hungry. "Especially when you're young, you're a lot more self-centered," he said in Vancouver on the eve of his 2006 charity game. "You don't see much farther than the reach of your arms and legs."

But the Santa Clara experience helped him tune into world issues and, when he became a wealthy young man playing in the NBA, it dawned on him: "I started to learn more about the diversity there is in the world and the inequality. It got me thinking. The NBA also does a great job in the community trying to bring people together. With those two forces, I realized I have the potential to help people individually, and it just kind of grew."

Nash's father, John, a friendly man who, like his wife, is immensely proud of all three of their children, often tells a story about Steve to illustrate his generosity. Some time ago, John noted to his eldest son that his foundation had already given away more than a half-million dollars. Steve replied, "Dad, think how much more we can give away."

Good buddy Al Whitley, who remembers Steve as that skinny little minor soccer superstar zooming across the neighborhood fields, marvels at the growth he has seen in his friend over the years.

"I think with his level of fame and fortune and the income that he's earned, he's able to touch a lot of people's lives and, you know, there are two things you can do when you get to that level," Whitley says. "You can keep it for yourself, or you can try to impact people's lives. And he's definitely just trying to help people out. He's done a phenomenal job in that way, something to be very proud of. He's very unselfish."

Steve is also true to his roots, taking the time to stay connected with many people from his past, despite the circles in which he is now traveling. For his charity game in Vancouver, he invited junior high coaches Dave Thomson and Mike Sheffer, elementary coach Mike Gallo, and former national team coaches Ken and Kathy Shields to steer the benches full of NBA players. It was a nice gesture to some of the people who helped him get where he is today.

"He's always been very loyal to his friends," Whitley says. "Through his continued success and his level of fame now, he still seems the same guy that he's always been. And I don't think that will ever change."

STEVE NASH: NBA CAREER STATISTICS

Year	Team	GP	MPG	FG%	3PT%	FT%	RPG	APG	PPG
1996–1997	Phoenix	65	10.5	.423	.418	.824	1.0	2.1	3.3
1997–1998	Phoenix	76	21.9	.459	.415	.860	2.1	3.4	9.1
1998–1999	Dallas	40	31.7	.363	.374	.826	2.9	5.5	7.9
1999–2000	Dallas	56	27.4	.477	.403	.882	2.2	4.9	8.6
2000–2001	Dallas	70	34.1	.487	.406	.895	3.2	7.3	15.6
2001–2002	Dallas	82	34.6	.483	.455	.887	3.1	7.7	17.9
2002–2003	Dallas	82	33.1	.465	.413	.909	2.9	7.3	17.7
2003–2004	Dallas	78	33.5	.470	.405	.916	3.0	8.8	14.5
2004–2005	Phoenix	75	34.3	.502	.431	.887	3.3	11.5	15.5
2005–2006	Phoenix	79	35.4	.512	.439	.921	4.2	10.5	18.8
Career	Phx/Dallas	703	30.0	.477	.421	.896	2.8	7.1	13.5
Playoffs	Phx/Dallas	86	36.0	.468	.411	.901	3.7	8.2	17.1

Legend: GP—games played; MPG—minutes per game; FG%—field goal percentage; 3PT%—three-point field goal percentage; FT%—free-throw percentage; RPG—rebounds per game; APG—assists per game; PPG—points per game

Source: www.nba.com/playerfile/steve_nash/index.html. © 2007 NBA Entertainment.

NBA AWARDS AND HIGHLIGHTS

NBA MVP
2004–2005, 2005–2006

All-NBA First Team
2004–2005, 2005–2006

All-NBA Third Team
2001–2002, 2002–2003

NBA Assists Leader
2004–2005, 2005–2006

NBA Free-Throw Leader
2005–2006

NBA All-Star Game Starter
2006

NBA All-Star Game Appearances
2002, 2003, 2005, 2006

Source: www.nba.com/playerfile/steve_nash/index.html

ACKNOWLEDGMENTS

A special thanks to the entire Nash family for their assistance, generosity, kindness, and co-operation with this project.

The author would also like to thank the following people and organizations for their assistance in the conception, writing, editing, and production of this project: Michelle Benjamin; Barbara Berson; Mark Cuban; Dick Davey; Bill Duffy; Julie Fie; Mike Gallo; Scott Gradin; the Dallas Mavericks; Dave Hutchings; Ian Hyde-Lay; Jenny Miller; Jean Nash; Joann Nash; John Nash; Steve Nash; Jennifer Notman; Penguin Canada; the Phoenix Suns; Lana, Maggie, and Matt Rud; St. Michaels University School; Santa Clara University Athletic Department; Mike Sheffer; Kathy and Ken Shields; The Steve Nash Foundation; Chris Talbott; Dave Thomson; Jay Triano; the Victoria *Times Colonist*; Brenda Waksel; Eric Walters; Al Whitley; Carroll Williams; and John Woolery.

Penguin Canada and the author would like to thank the following people for granting interviews used in the research and writing of this book: Steve Nash; John and Jean Nash; Mark Cuban; Ian Hyde-Lay; Al Whitley; Dick Davey; Scott Gradin; Dave Thomson; Mike Gallo; John Woolery; Ken Shields; Dave Hutchings; Carroll Williams; Jay Triano; and Bill Duffy.

Special thanks to the Ruds at Lake Cowichan and the Flavel crew at Nukko Lake for providing perfect getaways for writing and relaxing.

The following publications and websites were consulted in the research and writing of this book: *The Arizona Republic;* Associated Press; Canadian Press; *The Dallas Morning News;* ESPN.com; Fort Worth *Star-Telegram; The Globe and Mail;* Knight-Ridder News; *Long Shot: Steve Nash's Journey to the NBA* (Jeff Rud); *Los Angeles Times; The Miami Herald;* NBA.com; St. Michaels University School 1991–92 Yearbook; *San Francisco Chronicle; The San Francisco Examiner; San Jose Mercury News; The Seattle Times; Skywalking: How 10 Young Basketball Stars Soared to the Pros* (Jeff Rud); *Sports Illustrated;* Stevenash.org; *Time* Magazine; *The Province* (Vancouver); *The Vancouver Sun;* and *Times Colonist.*